T0288286

CONCISE
LINCOLN
LIBRARY

—

EDITED BY RICHARD W. ETULAIN,
SARA VAUGHN GABBARD, AND
SYLVIA FRANK RODRIGUE

MICHAEL BURLINGAME

Lincoln and the Civil War

Southern Illinois University Press
Carbondale and Edwardsville

14 13 12 11   4 3 2 1

The Concise Lincoln Library has been made possible
in part through a generous donation by the Leland E.
and LaRita R. Boren Trust.

Library of Congress Cataloging-in-Publication Data
Burlingame, Michael, 1941–
Lincoln and the Civil War / Michael Burlingame.
    p. cm. — (Concise Lincoln library)
Includes bibliographical references and index.
ISBN-13: 978-0-8093-3053-9 (cloth : alk. paper)
ISBN-10: 0-8093-3053-9 (cloth : alk. paper)
ISBN-13: 978-0-8093-9070-0 (ebook)
ISBN-10: 0-8093-9070-1 (ebook)
1. Lincoln, Abraham, 1809–1865. 2. Lincoln, Abraham,
1809–1865—Military leadership. 3. Presidents—Unit-
ed States—Biography. 4. United States—History—
Civil War, 1861–1865. 5. United States—Politics and
government—1861–1865. I. Title.
E457.B954 2011
973.7092—dc22   2010054551

Printed on recycled paper. ♻
The paper used in this publication meets the minimum
requirements of American National Standard for Information Sciences—Permanence of Paper for Printed
Library Materials, ANSI Z39.48-1992. ∞

For Dick and Ann Hart
with respect, affection, and gratitude

CONTENTS

LINCOLN AND THE CIVIL WAR

INTRODUCTION

If the legendary oddsmaker Jimmy the Greek had been alive when the Civil War began, he would probably have given the South a better-than-even chance of winning. As historian William Hanchett has cogently argued, "Contrary to the conventional assumption, the North, not the South, was the underdog in the Civil War."[1] To be sure, the North enjoyed obvious advantages: its industrializing economy was far more productive and diversified than the South's largely agricultural economy; moreover, 3,778,000 white males between the ages of eighteen and forty-five lived in the free states, while only 1,116,000 resided in the slave states.

But smaller nations have defeated larger ones in war. The American colonies won their independence from Great Britain, just as the Dutch won theirs from Spain. More recently, North Vietnam prevailed over the United States in the Vietnam War.

The South enjoyed many advantages that offset the North's economic might and greater population. To win, the North had to conquer the South, whereas the South merely had to fend off the North. It was widely assumed that attacking forces must enjoy at least a four-to-one advantage over their enemies in order to prevail. Because the South was a more militant region than the North, its army officers were generally more capable than their Northern counterparts, and Southern enlisted men had more experience with firearms, were more inured to hard riding, and had grown up more accustomed to outdoor life than Northern men. Since the war would be fought largely on

Southern soil, Confederates could take advantage of interior lines and shift their forces around more swiftly than the North could. In addition, Southerners were more familiar with the terrain where battles would take place, and they would have excellent sources of information about Yankee movements.

The Confederates' morale would be extremely high, for they would be repelling men they regarded as invaders and fighting for what they considered as the principles of the American Revolution.

Military technology favored Southerners, for they would be fighting on the defensive at a time when rifles were replacing smoothbore muskets. With their grooved barrels, rifles were far more accurate and had much greater range than muskets, thus giving defenders a significant advantage over attackers.

European nations would probably support the Confederacy in order to maintain access to Southern cotton, so vital to the British and French textile industries.

To conduct a mighty enterprise like the Civil War, the North would need an efficient, large-scale governmental apparatus that could mobilize its men and resources. In April 1861, the small, creaky bureaucratic structures of the federal government hardly fit that description. Nor was the civilian sector a model of organizational sophistication.

In order for the North to bring to bear its advantages, it would have to remain unified. Kentucky slaveholders must be kept in harness with Northern abolitionists; prohibitionists in Maine must work in tandem with beer-loving Germans in the Midwest; racial egalitarians in New England must make common cause with racists in most other states; free traders must compromise with protectionists; former Whigs must work closely with former Democrats. Unless those volatile elements in the unstable Republican coalition cooperated with each other, the South might well prevail.

Thus, Confederate General P. G. T. Beauregard had good reason to claim that "[n]o people ever warred for independence with more relative advantages than the Confederates." Years after the war, he recalled that Confederates "were one in sentiment as in territory, starting out, not with a struggling administration of doubtful authority, but with our ancient State governments and a fully organized central government." At the beginning of the war, the "South, with its great material resources, its defensive means of mountains, rivers, railroads, and telegraph, with the immense advantage of interior lines of war" was well positioned to win.[2]

If the North's advantages in manpower and economic resources were insufficient to assure its victory in the war, what was the critical variable that made that victory possible? Eminent historians agree that it was Abraham Lincoln's leadership. A century ago, Northern-born James Ford Rhodes, a Bourbon Democrat and author of the multivolume *History of the United States from the Compromise of 1850 to the Final Restoration of Home Rule at the South in 1877*, concluded that the "preponderating asset of the North proved to be Lincoln."[3] A generation later, James G. Randall, a partisan Midwestern Democrat who wrote a four-volume study, *Lincoln the President*, thought it "doubtful whether any other leader of the North could have matched him [Lincoln] in dramatizing the war to the popular mind, in shaping language to his purpose, in smoothing domestic and international complications, in courageously persisting in the face of almost unendurable discouragements, in maintaining war morale while refusing to harbor personal malice against the South."[4]

In 1960, Southern-born David M. Potter, author of *The Impending Crisis, 1848–1861*, speculated that "it hardly seems unrealistic to suppose that if the Union and the Confederacy had exchanged presidents with one another, the Confederacy might have won its independence." Potter asked, "In this sense, is it not justifiable that the overwhelming statistical advantages of the North predestined the Confederacy to defeat? Historians have never developed a really satisfactory way of dealing with the relationship between the vast, impersonal, long-range social and economic forces of history and the immediate, close-range, somewhat accidental factors of personality; but here is certainly a case where the factors of personality played an important part in guiding the impact of the impersonal social and economic forces."[5]

The contrast between the leadership of Lincoln and Jefferson Davis was stark indeed. As James M. McPherson, author of *The Battle Cry of Freedom: The Civil War Era*, put it: "a broad consensus exists that Lincoln was more eloquent than Davis in expressing war aims, more successful in communicating with the people, more skillful as a political leader in keeping factions working together for the war effort, better able to endure criticism and work with his critics to achieve a common goal."[6]

The personality differences between Lincoln and Davis were striking. Like many another politician, Davis was thin-skinned, taking criticism and disagreement personally. As a result, he quarreled with his vice president, his cabinet, his generals, his Congress, Southern newspaper editors, and the governors of Confederate states. Davis's prickly egotism and disputatious nature thus helped undermine Confederate unity.

Lincoln, on the other hand, managed to overcome the petty tyranny of the ego and to attain a level of psychological maturity, wholeness, and rootedness unmatched in the history of American public life. His extraordinary psychological consciousness equipped him to suppress his own personal feelings in pursuit of the central goal: victory in the war. Demonstrating preternatural self-control, he tolerated the snubs of condescending generals like George B. McClellan; the hostile machinations of contemptuous cabinet members like Salmon P. Chase; the haughtiness of senators like Charles Sumner; the insults of political opponents like Maryland Congressman Henry Winter Davis; the savage cries of Democratic newspaper editors, like Marcus "Brick" Pomeroy, who called for his assassination; and the patronizing attitude of Republican editors who kept second-guessing him, like Horace Greeley of the influential *New York Tribune*.

Lincoln refused to quarrel with such people for, as one of his closest friends observed: "He managed his politics upon a plan entirely different from any other man the country has ever produced. . . . In his conduct of the war he acted upon the theory that but one thing was necessary, and that was a united North. He had all the shades of sentiments and opinions to deal with, and the consideration was always presented to his mind: How can I hold these discordant elements together?"[7]

Lincoln was one of those rare men who are capable not only of giving good advice but also of acting on it. A case in point is the gentle but firm chastisement he gave to a Union captain who was squabbling with his superior officers. In 1863, Lincoln offered some wise paternal counsel to the young man. In doing so, he quoted from one of his favorite plays, Shakespeare's *Hamlet*: "The advice of a father to his son 'Beware of entrance to a quarrel, but being in, bear it that the opposed may beware of thee,' is good, and yet not the best. Quarrel not at all. No man resolved to make the most of himself, can spare time for personal contention. Still less can he afford to take all the consequences, including the vitiating of his temper, and the loss of self-control. Yield larger things to which you can show no more than equal right; and yield lesser ones, though clearly your own. Better give your path to a dog, than be bitten by him in contesting for the right. Even killing the dog would not cure the bite."[8] As president, Lincoln quarreled not at all. As he said a few months before his death, "So long as I have been here [in Washington] I have not willingly planted a thorn in any man's bosom."[9]

But as a young man, Lincoln had regularly planted thorns in other men's bosoms, especially those of his political opponents. During his twenties and thirties, Lincoln had been something of a political hack, taking the low road of personal invective, pouring sarcasm and ridicule over Democrats. He did not invent that form of political discourse—it was common on the frontier—but he was an unusually good practitioner. At times his remarks wounded his victims deeply. One of them, Jesse B. Thomas, left the debating platform in tears; another, James Shields, challenged Lincoln to a duel (which almost took place).[10]

But in his early forties, Lincoln underwent a profound transformation as he passed through a difficult, painful but ultimately positive midlife crisis. For the five years between 1849 and 1854, he sat on the political sidelines. In the preceding seventeen years, he had sought political office at every electoral cycle, but suddenly he stopped; he also campaigned for other candidates far less often and less enthusiastically than he had done earlier. "I was losing interest in politics" and "went to the practice of law with greater earnestness than ever before," he recalled. By 1854, the legal profession "had almost superseded the thought of politics" in his mind.[11]

During his semi-retirement from politics, Lincoln outwardly devoted himself to his law practice while inwardly wrestling with the profound questions that many men confront as they make the transition from early adulthood to middle adulthood: What do I really want from life? Is the structure of my life so far truly satisfactory? What kind of legacy do I wish to leave? Have I paid too much attention to the demands of the collective and conformed too much to its pressures? What do I hope to accomplish with the rest of my days? What do I really care about most? What are my basic beliefs? How have I failed to live up to the dream I formed years ago? How can I realistically modify that dream? Have I chosen the right career and the right spouse?[12]

A sense of failure often prompts such introspection, and in his forties, Lincoln was clearly ruminating on failure. "With *me*, the race of ambition has been a failure—a flat failure," he wrote in 1856.[13] A political ally noted that by that year, Lincoln had suffered many setbacks: "He went into the Black Hawk war as a captain, and . . . came out a private. He rode to the hostile frontier on horseback, and trudged home on foot. His store 'winked out.' His surveyor's compass and chain, with which he was earning a scanty living, were sold for debt. He was defeated in his first campaign for the legislature—defeated in his first attempt as a candidate for Congress. Four times he was defeated as a candidate for Presidential Elector, because the Whigs of Illinois were yet in a hopeless minority. He was defeated in his application to be appointed Commissioner of the General Land Office."[14] In 1857, a Democratic newspaper in Illinois remarked, "Lincoln is undoubtedly the most unfortunate politician that has ever attempted to rise in Illinois. In everything he undertakes, politically, he seems doomed to failure. He has been prostrated often enough in his political schemes to have crushed the life out of any ordinary man."[15] His law partner William H. Herndon recalled that Lincoln was "keenly sensitive to his failures," and the mere mention of them rendered him "miserable."[16] Remarking on his career at the bar, Lincoln confessed, "I am not an accomplished lawyer. I find quite as much material for a lecture, in those points where I have failed, as in those wherein I have been moderately successful."[17] In

1855, he said "with much feeling" that "men are greedy to publish the success of [their] efforts, but meanly shy as to publishing the failures of men. Men are ruined by this one sided practice of concealment of blunders and failures."[18]

During his early forties, Lincoln gave much thought to the legacy he wished to leave. In 1851, he lamented to his partner, "How hard—oh how more than hard, it is to die and leave one's Country no better for the life of him that lived and died her child."[19] Lincoln's best friend, Joshua Speed, recollected a similar statement: "He said to me he had done nothing to make any human being remember that he had lived—and that to connect his name with the events transpiring in his day & generation and so impress himself upon them, as to link his name to something that would redound to the interest of his fellow man was what he desired to live for."[20]

Like many men, Lincoln during his early forties became more aware of his mortality than he had been before. To be sure, he had long been death-obsessed. When he was a lad of nine, his mother died, along with her foster parents. His brother died in infancy when Abe was only two. His only other sibling, an older sister named Sarah, died when he was an adolescent. His sweetheart Ann Rutledge died when he was twenty-six. In 1850, his second son, three-year-old Eddie, died. In 1851, Lincoln's father, Thomas, passed away. As the old man lay dying in a town only a day's journey from Springfield, Lincoln coldly spurned his appeal for a deathbed visit. Lincoln asked his stepbrother to inform Thomas "that if we could meet now, it is doubtful whether it would not be more painful than pleasant."[21]

For some men, midlife introspection leads to despair; in others, it results in stagnation. In yet others, it can generate profound psychological growth, leading to a new awareness of one's own unique identity, and such awareness can strengthen self-confidence and inspire the confidence of others. Men who achieve this special psychological maturity are able to suppress their egos, to stop taking criticism and disagreement personally, to acknowledge calmly their own weaknesses and the shortcomings of others, and to relinquish things appropriate for youth and accept uncomplainingly the advantages and disadvantages of age. Men who undergo such growth in midlife attain a form of psychological wholeness and rootedness that commands respect. They become the unique individuals that they were meant to be.

During his early forties, Lincoln evolved into such a man, resembling the Kentuckian whom Ralph Waldo Emerson described in a lecture that Lincoln admired. The Sage of Concord noted that the bearing of men from the Bluegrass State radiated a message: "Here I am, if you don't like me, the worse for you."[22] During his last eleven years, Lincoln manifested what Herndon called "that peculiar nature . . . which distinguishes one person from another, as much to say 'I am myself and not you.'"[23] Speed observed that "if I was asked what it was that threw such charm around him, I would say it was his perfect naturalness. He could act no part but his own. He copied no one either in manner or style."[24] Lincoln "had no affectation in any thing," Speed remembered. "True to nature[,] true to himself, he was true to every body and every thing about and around him—When he was ignorant on any subject[,] no matter how simple[,] it might make him appear he was always willing to acknowledge it—His whole aim in life was to be true to himself & being true to himself he could be false to no one."[25] In 1859, a political ally wrote that what Lincoln "does and says is all his own. What William Henry Seward and others do you feel that you have read in books or speeches, or that it is a sort of deduction from what the world is full of. But what Lincoln does you feel to be something newly mined out—something above the ordinary."[26] John H. Littlefield, who studied in the Lincoln-Herndon law office in the late 1850s, recalled that Lincoln "was a very modest man in his demeanor, and yet gave you an impression of strong individuality. In his freedom of intercourse with people he would seem to put himself of a par with everybody; and yet there was within him a sort of reserved power, a quiet dignity which prevented people from presuming on him, notwithstanding he had thrown down the social bars. A person of less individuality would have been trifled with."[27]

Lincoln also had a quality that some observers called "psychic radiance."[28] A close friend, Joseph Gillespie, recalled seeing him in 1858 at Highland, Illinois, where residents flocked to greet him:

"there was some magnetic influence at work that was perfectly inexplicable, which brought him & the masses into a mysterious correspondence with each other." Over time, Gillespie noted, that "relation increased and was intensified to such an extent that afterwards at Springfield I witnessed a manifestation of regard for Mr. Lincoln, such as I did not suppose was possible."[29] Lincoln's voice and presence helped create that "magnetic influence." Henry C. Whitney, a colleague at the bar, found it hard to describe Lincoln's uniqueness. Though he was "awkward and ungainly," Whitney wrote, "there nevertheless was in his *tout ensemble* an indefinable *something* that commanded respect."[30]

In 1863, Jane Grey Swisshelm, a Radical critic of Lincoln, called on him "with a feeling of scorn for the man who had tried to save the Union and slavery." But soon she was "startled to find a chill of awe pass over me as my eyes rested upon him. It was as if I had suddenly passed a turn in a road and come into full view of the Matterhorn. . . . I have always been sensitive to the atmosphere of those I meet, but have never found that of any one impress me as did that of Mr. Lincoln, and I know no word save 'grandeur' which expresses the quality of that atmosphere."[31] An Illinois railroad conductor who over the years had observed many eminent politicians described Lincoln as "the most folksy of them. He put on no airs. He did not hold himself distant from any man." Yet "there was something about him which we plain people couldn't explain that made us stand a little in awe of him. . . . You could get near him in a sort of neighborly way, as though you had always known him, but there was something tremendous between you and him all the time."[32]

Lincoln's folksy modesty was no affectation. Like most people who have acknowledged their own dark side, he entertained no high opinion of his own virtue. "I am very sure," he confided to a friend one day in the White House, "that if I do not go away from here a wiser man, I shall go away a better man, for having learned here what a very poor sort of a man I am."[33] To a group of clergymen who called on him during the Civil War, he acknowledged, "I may not be a great man—(straightening up to his full height) I know I am not a great man."[34]

And yet Lincoln was remarkably self-confident. In 1863, impressed by the president's lack of egotism, John Hay wrote in his diary: "While the rest are grinding their little private organs for their own glorification the old man is working with the strength of a giant and the purity of an angel to do this great work."[35] When Lincoln used the first-person-singular pronoun, he did not sound egocentric. The poet James Russell Lowell, commenting on the president's "unconsciousness of self," remarked that he "forgets himself so entirely in his object as to give his *I* the sympathetic and persuasive effect of *We* with the great body of his countrymen." The effect, said Lowell, was that "when he speaks, it seems as if the people were listening to their own thinking aloud."[36]

Lincoln's psychological maturity and profound humility, along with his self-awareness and self-confidence, enabled him to pilot the North to victory in the Civil War. The journalist Horace White, a leader of the Illinois Republican Party, was amazed at the way that "Lincoln quickly gained the confidence of strangers, and . . . their affection as well. I found myself strongly drawn to him from the first. . . . This personal quality, whose influence I saw growing and widening among the people of Illinois from day to day, eventually penetrated to all the Northern States. . . . It was his magical personality that commanded all loyal hearts. It was his leadership that upheld confidence in the dark hours of the war and sent back to the White House the sublime refrain, 'We are coming, Father Abraham, three hundred thousand more.'"[37]

If Lincoln had been less psychologically mature, the failings of ordinary humanity—egotism, envy, jealousy, self-righteousness, false pride, vanity—would have undermined his capacity for maintaining Northern unity and resolve. To meet that challenge required what one caller termed Lincoln's "transparent honesty, his republican simplicity, his gushing sympathy for those who offered their lives for their country, his utter *forgetfulness of self* in his concern for his country,"[38] and such forgetfulness—the ability to ignore the clamorous demands of the ego—Lincoln developed after he had successfully come to grips with the challenges of midlife.

THE ELECTION OF 1860 AND
SOUTHERN SECESSION

L incoln's victory in the 1860 election, which precipitated the Civil War, was both a referendum on slavery and a repudiation of the corrupt administrations of Democratic Presidents Franklin Pierce (1853–57) and James Buchanan (1857–61). Shortly after his electoral triumph, Lincoln said, "I have been elected mainly on the cry 'Honest Old Abe.'"[1] Abundant evidence suggests that he was right. Voters' desire for honesty in government played a key role at the polls in November. The public was fed up with steamship lobbies, land-grant bribery, hireling journalists, the spoils system, rigged political conventions, and cost overruns on government projects. Buchanan and Pierce had offended the electorate by tolerating such abuses of power. To punish the Democrats, citizens decided to throw the rascals out and elect Lincoln, not so much because he championed the antislavery cause but rather because he was perceived to be a man of integrity.

Many voters shared Indiana Congressman David Kilgore's desire "to see this *God forsaken Hell deserving* set of corrupt politicians turned out of office, and honest men put in their places."[2] Among those voters was a New Englander who explained, "Multitudes of us voted the republican ticket because we wanted *honesty* to displace corruption."[3] Another was the New York economist David A. Wells: "I voted for Mr. Lincoln, not because I hated slavery, or thought it a sin, or wished in any way to do my neighbor a wrong,—but because I was disgusted with the present Administration, & wished for a change."[4] In Rhode Island, a Democrat concluded that Republican success "is not owing to anti-slavery; it is owing to the failure of the Democratic federal administration,—a failure caused by corruption and one-sidedness and an ultra pro-slavery policy." He added that if Buchanan had "been honest and able, the Republicans would have been badly beaten."[5] Horace Greeley, editor of the most influential Northern Republican newspaper, the *New York Tribune*, doubted that many Northerners hated slavery on moral grounds and insisted that they desired above all things "*a Radical reform in the patronage and expenditures of the Government.*"[6]

On election eve, the *New York World* remarked that many thousand "intelligent men support the candidates of the republican party, not that they care a broken tobacco-pipe for the negro question, but because they see no other way to honest management at Washington. They believe that the democratic party has been so long in power that it has become corrupt; that it understands too well the crooked arts by which partizan pockets are lined at the public expense; and that it is safer to try an experiment with new men and a young party, than to continue a set of old party hacks at the public crib. If Mr. Lincoln's administration shall prove honest, economical and tranquillizing, they will be quite satisfied, though he should never once allude to free soil in any of his annual messages."[7]

Many Southerners, however, did not view Lincoln's election as a routine exercise in turning out corrupt rascals. Instead, they perceived the Republican standard bearer as a wolf in sheep's clothing, a John Brown–style radical abolitionist who pretended to be only a moderate opponent of slavery expansion. They did not believe his protestations that he would not touch slavery where it existed. His famous 1858 House Divided address they interpreted as a call for war against the South. They were alarmed by another speech he gave that year in which he declared: "let us discard all this quibbling about this man and the other man—this race and that race and the other race being inferior, and therefore they must be placed in an inferior position. . . . Let us discard all these things, and unite as one people throughout this land, until we shall once more stand up declaring that all men are created equal."[8] Such egalitarian rhetoric affronted the millions of Southerners whose devotion to white supremacy formed the core of their identity.

When assured that Lincoln was a moderate Republican who would leave slavery intact in the fifteen states where it already existed, Southerners replied that his election foreshadowed the doom of slavery nonetheless, for he and his party opposed any expansion of the peculiar institution. As a South Carolina theologian put it, "There are no objections to him as a man, or as a citizen of the North. He is probably entitled, in the private relations of life, to all the commendations which his friends have bestowed upon him."[9] Similarly, a North Carolina Unionist wrote, "It is not Lincoln—so far as he is concerned, he is taken but little in the account. . . . But it is . . . the *fundamental idea*, that underlies the whole movement of his nomination, the canvass, & his election. It is the declaration of unceasing warfare against slavery as an institution."[10]

And so, in the months immediately following Lincoln's election, the seven states of the Lower South (South Carolina, Georgia, Florida, Alabama, Mississippi, Louisiana, and Texas) seceded from the Union. They did so mainly to protect slavery and thereby preserve white supremacy.[11] In February 1861, they banded together to form the Confederate States of America. Their vice president, Alexander H. Stephens of Georgia, explained that the Confederacy's "foundations are laid, its corner-stone rests upon the great truth, that the negro is not equal to the white man; that slavery—subordination to the superior race—is his natural and normal condition. This, our new government, is the first, in the history of the world, based upon this great physical, philosophical, and moral truth." Thomas Jefferson and other Founding Fathers had based the Declaration of Independence and the Constitution "upon the assumption of the equality of races. This was an error."[12] Shortly after his state seceded, another Georgian maintained that the "institution of African Slavery produced the Secession of the Cotton States. If it had never existed, the Union of the States would, to-day, be complete. But, by the existence of African Slavery in the Southern States, civilization has arrived at a degree of perfection equal to that of any age in the history of the world."[13] Early in the Civil War, a Confederate in Florida stated bluntly that the "very thing we are fighting for is the privilege of doing what we please with our niggers."[14]

In addition, Southerners seceded because Republicans hurt their feelings by criticizing slavery. Louisiana Senator Judah P. Benjamin denounced "the incessant attack of the Republicans, not simply on the interests, but on the feelings and sensibilities of a high-spirited people by the most insulting language, and the most offensive epithets."[15] As a New Orleans editor put it, his region "has been moved to resistance chiefly . . . by the popular dogma in the free states that slavery is a crime in the sight of GOD. The South in the eyes of the North, is degraded and unworthy, because of the institution of servitude."[16]

Southerners also thought it unmanly to acquiesce in the Republicans' demand that slavery be barred from the territories. That prohibition they termed, in the words of a leading fire-eater, William L. Yancey, "discrimination as degrading as it is injurious to the slaveholding states."[17] In May 1860, John Bell of Tennessee, presidential candidate of the Constitutional Union party, speculated that "the whole South, in 30 days after the election of 'Lincoln' would feel his election to be an *insult* to them."[18] Southern indignation at discriminatory legislation had emerged in 1846, when Congress debated the Wilmot Proviso, which would have excluded slavery from any territory acquired from Mexico as a result of the war then underway. Commenting on the proposed legislation, U.S. Supreme Court Justice Peter V. Daniel, a Virginian, said, "There is another aspect of this pretension now advanced, which exhibits it as fraught with dangers far greater than any that can flow from mere calculations of political influence, or profit, arising from a distribution of territory. It is that view of the case which pretends to an insulting exclusiveness or superiority on the one hand, and denounces a degrading inequality or inferiority on the other: which says in effect to the Southern man, Avaunt! You are not my equal and hence are to be excluded as carrying a moral taint with you. Here is at once the extinction of all fraternity, of all sympathy of all endurance even: the creation of animosity fierce, implacable, undying. It is the immitigable outrage, which I venture to say, there is no true Southron from the schoolboy to the octogenarian, who is not prepared for any extremity in order to repel it."[19] In 1850, Mississippi Senator Jefferson Davis, future president of the Confederacy, declared that Southerners would become "an inferior class, a degraded class in the Union" if they could not take their slaves into the territories.[20]

As president-elect, Lincoln resisted pressure to appease secessionists. The Republican Party, he insisted, had won the election fairly; it had made clear its opposition to slavery expansion. If Republicans backed down in the face of Southern threats to dissolve the Union, they would undermine the principle of majority rule. Lincoln argued that "when ballots have fairly, and constitutionally decided [an election]," then "there can be no successful appeal, except to ballots themselves, at succeeding elections." When timid Republicans urged passage of the so-called Crittenden Compromise, which would have allowed slavery to expand south of the latitude 36° 30′, Lincoln emphatically rebuffed them.[21] In early December 1860, Lincoln told Illinois Congressman William Kellogg, "Entertain no proposition for a compromise in regard to the *extension* of slavery. The instant you do, they have us under again; all our labor is lost, and sooner or later must be done over. . . . The tug has to come & better now than later."[22] Two days later, Lincoln urged another Illinois congressman to "[p]revent, as far as possible, any of our friends from demoralizing themselves, and our cause, by entertaining propositions for compromise of any sort, on '*slavery extention*.' There is no possible compromise upon it, but which puts us under again, and leaves all our work to do over again. . . . On that point hold firm, as with a chain of steel."[23]

Lincoln's stern opposition to the Crittenden Compromise helped defeat it. On December 22, the Senate Committee of Thirteen turned it down, and the full Senate followed suit on January 16. Massachusetts Congressman Charles Francis Adams observed that the "declarations coming almost openly from Mr Lincoln have had the effect of perfectly consolidating the Republicans."[24] Another Bay State legislator wrote that some congressional Republicans "are weak; most of them are firm. Lincoln's firmness helps our weak ones [stay firm]."[25]

Lincoln's decision to resist Senator Crittenden's scheme was fateful, for that compromise proposal, despite its many practical problems and its silence on the constitutionality of secession and the right of a legally elected president to govern, represented the best hope of placating the Upper South and thus of possibly averting war. That was a forlorn hope at best, however, given the intransigence of Southern legislators. Even in the face of Lincoln's opposition, the House Committee of Thirty-Three might have approved Crittenden's plan if Democrats had not insisted that slavery be protected south of the 36° 30' line in all future acquisitions as well as in territory already part of the United States. Though Senate Republicans rejected the compromise, it still could have passed the upper house on January 16 if three of the six Southern senators in attendance had voted for it instead of abstaining; similarly, if two abstaining Democratic senators on the Committee of Thirteen (established to consider possible compromises) had voted on December 22 for Crittenden's handiwork, it would have received the endorsement of that body. Thus, to argue that the Civil War was the result of Lincoln's opposition to the Crittenden Compromise—as did some contemporaries and some later historians—hardly seems justified.[26]

Lincoln has also been criticized for his failure during the months following his election to reassure the South of his peaceful intentions. But that criticism, too, is questionable. In late November, Lincoln penned some soothing remarks for his friend Illinois Senator Lyman Trumbull to deliver: "I have labored in, and for, the Republican organization with entire confidence that whenever it shall be in power, each and all of the States will be left in as complete control of their own affairs respectively, and at as perfect liberty to choose, and employ, their own means of protecting property, and preserving peace and order within their respective limits, as they have ever been under any administration. Those who have voted for Mr. Lincoln, have expected, and still expect this; and they would not have voted for him had they expected otherwise. I regard it as extremely fortunate for the peace of the whole country, that this point, upon which the Republicans have been so long, and so persistently misrepresented, is now to be brought to a practical test, and placed beyond the possibility of doubt. Disunionists per se, are now in hot haste to get out of the Union, precisely because they perceive they can not, much longer, maintain apprehension among the Southern people that their homes, and firesides, and lives, are to be endangered by the action of the Federal Government. With such '*Now, or never*' is the maxim." Lincoln added a naïve closing remark: "I am rather glad of this military preparation in the South. It will enable the people the more easily to suppress any uprisings there, which their misrepresentations of purposes may have encouraged."[27]

The press soon reported Lincoln's authorship of these words. The reaction to them confirmed his belief that he should not speak out. Though Republican newspapers sang Trumbull's praises, Democratic papers failed to do so. And so Lincoln told the editor of the *New York Times*: "On the 20th. inst. Senator Trumbull made a short speech which I suppose you have both seen and approved. Has a single newspaper, heretofore against us, urged that speech [upon its readers] with a purpose to quiet public anxiety? Not one, so far as I know. On the contrary the [Democratic] Boston Courier, and its' class, hold me responsible for the speech, and endeavor to inflame the North with the belief that it foreshadows an abandonment of Republican ground by the incoming administration; while the Washington Constitution, and its' class hold the same speech up to the South as an open declaration of war against them. This is just as I expected, and just what would happen with any declaration I could make."[28]

But Lincoln did seek to placate Southerners by appointing men from slave states to his cabinet. He approached John A. Gilmer of North Carolina, one of the few Southern congressmen to vote against the 1857 Lecompton Constitution, which proslavery forces in the Kansas Territory had adopted by fraudulent means. Gilmer, evidently fearing the disapproval of fellow Tarheels if he should associate himself with a Republican administration, declined Lincoln's offer.

Lincoln sounded out other Southern leaders, including another North Carolinian, William A. Graham, who expressed no interest, and James Guthrie of Kentucky, who refused. Frustrated, Lincoln published an anonymous query in the Springfield *Illinois State Journal*: "We see such frequent allusion to a supposed purpose on the part of Mr. Lincoln to call into his cabinet two or three Southern gentlemen, from the parties opposed to him politically, that we are prompted to ask a few questions.

"1st. Is it known that any such gentleman of character, would accept a place in the cabinet?

"2—If yea, on what terms? Does he surrender to Mr. Lincoln, or Mr. Lincoln to him, on the political difference between them? Or do they enter upon the administration in open opposition to each other?"[29]

The *Journal* also ran a passage from Lincoln's 1858 House Divided speech: "Our cause, then, must be intrusted to, and conducted by, *its own undoubted friends*."[30] To Missouri Congressman Frank Blair, Lincoln remarked that "he could hardly maintain his self respect" if he appointed a Southern opponent to his cabinet for "he considered such a course an admission that the Republican party was incapable of governing the country & would be a rebuke by him to those who had voted for him."[31] He hesitated to offer a cabinet position to men from the Deep South, for fear that "they might decline, with insulting letters still further inflaming the public mind."[32]

To placate Southerners, eventually Lincoln settled on two men from Border States, Edward Bates of Missouri and Montgomery Blair of Maryland. The former became attorney general and the latter postmaster general.

The other five men chosen for the cabinet were Northerners: William Henry Seward of New York (secretary of state), Salmon P. Chase of Ohio (secretary of the treasury), Caleb B. Smith of Indiana (secretary of the interior), Simon Cameron of Pennsylvania (secretary of war), and Gideon Welles of Connecticut (secretary of the navy).

Lincoln did not fear being overshadowed by these men, four of whom had been aspirants for the Republican presidential nomination. Seward and Chase were especially strong-willed leaders, with powerful political constituencies and impressive resumes. When warned that Chase regarded himself as "a great deal bigger" than the president-elect, Lincoln replied, "Well, do you know of any other men who think they are bigger than I am? I want to put them all in my cabinet."[33] Lincoln's decision to name his rivals to the cabinet demonstrated exceptional self-confidence. He felt no need to appoint sycophants who would depend on him for political advancement; rather, he picked leaders with big personalities, outsized egos, and influential followings whose support he deemed essential for the success of his administration.

In selecting Cameron to serve as secretary of war, Lincoln indicated that he did not expect hostilities to break out. Cameron was a shrewd political operator "whose very name stinks in the nostrils of the people for his corruption," as Lincoln remarked.[34] Without Lincoln's authorization, his managers at the Republican convention had virtually promised a cabinet post to Cameron, who cleverly lined up support for his own candidacy. Opponents, however, had deluged Lincoln with abundant evidence of Cameron's shortcomings, and it therefore seems unlikely that the Pennsylvania boss would have received the portfolio of the war department if the president-elect thought civil war was imminent.

Some presidents, like Franklin D. Roosevelt, have chosen coalition cabinets to help maintain national unity in wartime. In 1940, Roosevelt appointed Frank Knox and Henry Stimson to his cabinet after war had broken out in Europe, and the United States seemed clearly destined to be dragged into the conflict. But it is unrealistic to imagine that Lincoln could have named someone like Stephen A. Douglas to his cabinet, given Douglas's hostility to Republican doctrine and his repeated assaults on Republican leaders. Knox and Stimson did not have the stature of Douglas, nor had they been such fierce opponents of Roosevelt as Douglas had been of Lincoln. Given the political climate during the winter of 1860–61, Lincoln went as far as reasonably could have been expected to form a coalition cabinet.

Like many other Northerners, Lincoln believed that Southern Unionism was so strong that the secession crisis could be peacefully solved. If only he could retain within the union the eight slave states of the Upper South and the Border region, then the seven states of the Lower South would eventually realize that their Confederacy was too small to flourish on its own, and they would therefore rejoin the Union voluntarily.

Lincoln had good reason to expect that the Upper South and Border States would not secede. A former Tennessee governor,

William B. Campbell, declared that secession was "unwise and impolitic" because it would hasten "the ruin and overthrow of negro slavery" and jeopardize "the freedom and liberty of the white men." Campbell predicted that his own state as well as Kentucky would not be "dragged into a rebellion that their whole population utterly disapproved."[35] The reluctance of the Upper South to follow the lead of the Cotton States baffled one Louisianan, who asked, "Is it not strange, when the border states suffer so much more from Northern fanaticism, from actual loss in their property, and these same states equally interested in slavery, that a feeling of antagonism to the North, should be so much stronger [in the Deep South]?"[36] Such reasonable men in the Upper South, Lincoln believed, would prevail over their more hotheaded neighbors.

Lincoln's optimism was also rooted in what he heard from many visitors who called on him in Springfield, from what he read in newspapers, and from his analysis of the 1860 election results. In the slave states, John C. Breckinridge, the Southern Democratic candidate favored by secessionists, received only 44 percent of the ballots cast. John Bell, the Constitutional Union candidate, and Stephen A. Douglas, the candidate of the Northern Democrats, both of whom opposed secession, together won 110,000 more Southern votes than did Breckinridge. Bell carried Virginia with 44 percent of the vote, Tennessee with 48 percent, Kentucky with 45 percent, and almost triumphed in North Carolina with 47 percent, Maryland with 45.15 percent (to Breckinridge's 45.92 percent), and Missouri with 35.3 percent (to Douglas's 35.5 percent). In those states, ex-Whigs felt uncomfortable allying with the Democrats whom they had fought against for decades.

Unionist sentiment seemed strong in the Upper South states of Virginia, North Carolina, Arkansas, and Tennessee, as well as in the Border States of Kentucky, Missouri, Delaware, and Maryland. Fewer slaves lived there than in the Deep South, and Whiggish sentiments and organizations were more persistent. The white population of the seven Deep South states was half the size of the white population of the eight other slave states. Southern Unionists detected few economic benefits in joining the Confederacy; they looked askance at prominent secessionists, who seemed like delusional conspirators bent on frightening their neighbors; they dreaded the prospect of hostilities resulting from a misunderstanding of Northern intentions; and they entertained the hope that Republicans might clear up that misunderstanding. Some were unconditional Unionists, requiring no Republicans concessions; most, however, were conditional Unionists, willing to resist secession so long as the federal government did not act against the Confederacy and so long as Republicans seemed willing to accept some compromise.

Lincoln evidently believed that if he could frame an inaugural address that was conciliatory enough for Southern Unionists, yet firm enough to satisfy Republican hard-liners, and then show the South by his actions—enforcing the Fugitive Slave Law, not interfering with slavery in the states where it existed, not appointing antislavery zealots to federal posts in the Southern states—that he was no John Brown, then the crisis would pass. Time would work its healing wonders. The Hotspurs of the Lower South would have sober second thoughts and rejoin the Union.

It was not an unreasonable expectation.

FROM ELECTION TO INAUGURATION

As President James Buchanan meekly allowed secessionists to seize federal facilities throughout the Lower South, Lincoln fumed. When told that the lame-duck chief executive might surrender Fort Moultrie at Charleston, South Carolina, Lincoln expostulated, "If that is true, they ought to hang him."[1] A visitor to Springfield thought that Lincoln's "Kentucky blood is up, he means *fight*."[2]

Many Northerners shared Lincoln's indignation; they regarded the Southern takeover of federal facilities as "gigantic robbery." Such action severely weakened Northern enthusiasm for any compromise.[3] John A. Dix of New York, Buchanan's secretary of the treasury during the winter of 1860–61, recalled that "the forcible seizure of arsenals, mints, revenue-cutters, and other property of the common government . . . aroused a feeling of exasperation which nothing but the arbitrament of arms could overcome."[4]

As Lincoln started composing his inaugural address, his anger prompted him to state: "All the power at my disposal will be used to reclaim the public property and places which have fallen; to hold, occupy and possess these, and all other property and places belonging to the government." But when friends warned that such a hard-line posture might impel the Upper South to join Confederacy, Lincoln toned down the sentence: "All the power at my disposal will be used to hold, occupy and possess the property and places belonging to the government."

But before he could deliver this more conciliatory version of his inaugural, Lincoln had to give many speeches on his twelve-day train journey from Springfield, Illinois, to Washington, D.C. The nation watched anxiously as he ended his months-long silence on the secession crisis. People wondered if he would be a hawk or a dove.

Alas, it was hard to tell, for Lincoln seemed to oscillate between firm insistence that he would retake federal property and conciliatory willingness to eschew aggressive action. At Indianapolis on February 11, Lincoln sounded hawkish as he parsed the words *coercion* and *invasion*. Rhetorically he asked a charged question: if the administration "simply insists upon holding its own forts, or retaking those forts which belong to it, or the enforcement of the laws of the United States in the collection of duties upon foreign importations, or even the withdrawal of the mails from those portions of the country where the mails themselves are habitually violated; would any or all of these things be coercion?"[5] To many Southerners, his words constituted a declaration of war against their section. Evidently taken aback by that reaction, Lincoln thereafter softened his rhetoric, stressing that he would treat the South fairly and playing down the seriousness of the crisis. But at Trenton, New Jersey, he reverted to his earlier tough line: "The man does not live who is more devoted to peace than I am. None who would do more to preserve it. But it may be necessary to put the foot down firmly."[6] A journalist recalled that in "the shouts and cheers and yells and shrieks," one "could hear not only the resolution of battle, but the belief that there was now going to be a fight. The South had bluffed so long" that the Republicans were finally "resolved on a war, and did not mean to waste any time about taking up the gage of battle."[7] The Lower South grew convinced that Lincoln's policies would produce a war that they felt confident they could win.

On February 23, Lincoln's arrival cheered up Washingtonians, though many observers were nervous because nobody knew what kind of compromise, if any, he would support. Cautiously, he tried to allay Southern fears. When it seemed likely that a hastily assembled peace conference would fail to reach agreement on a compromise, he evidently persuaded the Illinois delegation to reverse its opposition to a plan resembling the Crittenden Compromise. The last-minute adoption of that proposal, which was to be submitted to Congress, caused Southern Unionists to rejoice. If the conference had come up empty-handed, some Upper South states may have seceded forthwith.

Lincoln took other steps to allay Southern fears. When Congress considered a "force bill" authorizing the president to take military measures to put down an insurrection, he worked behind the scenes to scuttle it. He also helped kill a measure providing for the offshore collection of tariff revenues. Reluctantly, he appointed to his cabinet Simon Cameron, who supported conciliation of the South. Moreover, Lincoln continued revising his inaugural address, making it ever less bellicose. In its final form, Lincoln stressed that his policy proposals were tentative: "So far as possible, the people everywhere shall have that sense of perfect security which is most favorable to calm thought and reflection. The course here indicated will be followed, unless current events, and experience, shall show a modification, or change, to be proper; and in every case and exigency, my best discretion will be exercised, according to circumstances actually existing, and with a view and a hope of a peaceful solution of the national troubles, and the restoration of paternal sympathies and, affections."[8]

Before inauguration day, Lincoln also made conciliatory public statements. On February 27, he told Mayor James G. Berret of Washington, D.C.: "I think very much of the ill feeling that has existed and still exists between the people of the section from whence I came and the people here, is owing to a misunderstanding between each other which unhappily prevails. I therefore avail myself of this opportunity to assure you, Mr. Mayor, and all the gentlemen present, that I have not now, and never have had, any other than as kindly feelings towards you as to the people of my own section. I have not now, and never have had, any disposition to treat you in any respect otherwise than as my own neighbors. I have not now any purpose to withhold from you any of the benefits of the constitution, under any circumstances, that I would not feel myself constrained to withhold from my own neighbors; and I hope, in a word, when we shall become better acquainted—and I say it with great confidence—we shall like each other the more."[9] In the days before the inauguration, Lincoln's conciliatory steps were taken partly because of William Henry Seward's urging and partly because of Lincoln's growing awareness of the depth of secessionist feeling in the Upper South and Border States.

While the president-elect was willing to follow Seward's advice, he was unwilling to let the secretary of state dominate the administration. Seward, the leading soft-liner, opposed the appointment of Chase, a prominent hard-liner. When Seward threatened at the last minute to withdraw his acceptance of a cabinet position, Lincoln successfully called his bluff. Lincoln did the same with Chase, who coyly hinted that he might not accept the treasury department portfolio.

On inauguration day, Lincoln offered two more olive branches to the South. One was his endorsement of a thirteenth constitutional amendment protecting slavery where it already existed: "No amendment shall ever be made to the Constitution which will authorize or give to Congress the power to abolish or interfere, within any State, with the domestic institutions thereof, including that of persons held to labor or service by the laws of said State." Eight hours before he addressed the nation, the Senate had passed the measure with a bare two-thirds majority, evidently thanks to Lincoln's intervention. On the night of March 3, he apparently lobbied senators on behalf of the measure without knowing its precise details. The other olive branch was Lincoln's proposal that the states call for a national constitutional convention. Those two concessions were as far as Lincoln could go without seeming to abandon his party's platform. He did insist that he would not support any expansion of slavery, nor would he admit that secession was legal.

Ten months later, when Ohio Congressman John A. Bingham mentioned to him the proposed thirteenth constitutional amendment, Lincoln said, "It is extraordinary that I should have made such statements in my Inaugural. Are you not mistaken about this?" To Bingham it seemed as if the president "felt that the proposed Amendment had not been correctly reported to him, and that some one had blundered. He reproached no one, nor did he intimate how or by whose agency this passage came to be in the Inaugural Address."[10] He probably thought an unamendable amendment was an oxymoron, that it was unconstitutional, and that it was a mere tautology, restating what was clearly implied in the Constitution. He doubtless viewed his support for the amendment, which had no chance of winning ratification, as a sop to Seward and his followers and to the Upper South and Border States. (Four years later, a different thirteenth amendment would be adopted, abolishing rather than guaranteeing slavery.)

The tone of the inaugural was conciliatory, thanks in part to Seward's suggestions. The secretary of state had proposed a clumsily worded closing paragraph stressing sectional fraternity. Like a rhetorical alchemist, Lincoln transformed Seward's leaden prose into golden poetry: "I am loth to close. We are not enemies, but friends. We must not be enemies. Though passion may have strained, it must not break our bonds of affection. The mystic chords of memory, stretching from every battlefield, and patriot grave, to every living heart and hearthstone, all over this broad land, will yet swell the chorus of the Union, when again touched, as surely they will be, by the better angels of our nature."[11]

Although the inaugural was not as conciliatory as Seward wanted it to be, it was tough without being belligerent. Lincoln clearly followed Seward's advice to soften the hard-line approach in early drafts of his inaugural, yet he emphatically rejected the doctrine of secession: "I hold that in contemplation of universal law, and of the Constitution, the Union of these States is perpetual." Therefore no state, "upon its own mere motion," could legally secede. "I therefore consider that, in view of the constitution and the laws, the Union is unbroken; and, to the extent of my ability, I shall take care, as the constitution itself expressly enjoins upon me, that the laws of the Union be faithfully executed in all the states. Doing this I deem to be only a simple duty on my part; and I shall perform it, so far as practicable, unless my rightful masters, the American people, shall withhold the requisite means, or, in some authoritative manner, direct the contrary. I trust this will not be regarded as a menace, but only as the declared purpose of the Union that it will constitutionally defend, and maintain itself. In doing this there needs to be no bloodshed or violence; and there shall be none, unless it be forced upon the national authority."[12]

If states could withdraw from the Union whenever they wanted to, the result would be chaos leading either to anarchy or to tyranny:

"Plainly, the central idea of secession, is the essence of anarchy. A majority, held in restraint by constitutional checks, and limitations, and always changing easily, with deliberate changes of popular opinions and sentiments, is the only true sovereign of a free people. Whoever rejects it, does, of necessity, fly to anarchy or to despotism. Unanimity is impossible; the rule of a minority, as a permanent arrangement, is wholly inadmissable; so that, rejecting the majority principle, anarchy, or despotism in some form, is all that is left."[13]

The most controversial sentence in the inaugural read: "The power confided to me, will be used to hold, occupy, and possess the property, and places belonging to the government, and to collect the duties and imposts; but beyond what may be necessary for these objects, there will be no invasion—no using of force against, or among the people anywhere."[14]

Across the nation, the address was eagerly read and heatedly discussed. Northerners tended to think that it was, as a New Hampshire native wrote, "conciliatory—peaceable—but firm in its tone, and is exactly what we, Union men, want."[15] Southerners, on the other hand, warned that if Lincoln did try to hold the Southern forts and to collect import duties, "there will be war—open, declared, positive war—with booming cannon and blood."[16] But in the Upper South and Border States, Unionists took heart, for both the tone and the substance of the inaugural seemed conciliatory and pacific.

Therefore, Lincoln might reasonably have anticipated a peaceable end to the secession crisis. His address evidently strengthened Southern Unionists. Time could now work its healing wonders. "Nothing valuable can be lost by taking time," he had stated in his inaugural. He assumed that Southerners would come to recognize that he was no John Brown in sheep's clothing; the Upper South and Border States would probably refuse to secede; the Lower South would sooner or later realize that it could not flourish as an independent nation and would therefore rejoin the Union. In May, Virginia voters might well send Unionists to Congress; in August, Tennessee, Kentucky, and North Carolina would probably do the same; in November, Maryland would follow suit. The nation would be restored without bloodshed.

THE FORT SUMTER CRISIS

Tragically, the time for reflection proved far shorter than Lincoln had anticipated. On March 5, 1861, a letter arrived at the White House demolishing his hopeful scenario. The commander of Fort Sumter in Charleston harbor, Major Robert Anderson, wrote saying that his men would exhaust their food supply within six weeks. The administration must either resupply them or surrender the garrison. The former option would probably lead to war, the latter to "national destruction."[1] Lincoln must choose between them and choose quickly.

In dealing with the Sumter crisis, Lincoln struggled with Secretary of State William Henry Seward, who considered himself a wise, venerable statesman responsible for helping the inexperienced president, eight years his junior, make sound policy decisions. Unlike Lincoln, Seward believed that the administration was not bound to honor the Republicans' Chicago platform and that shrewd intrigue and clever maneuvering could overcome Southern disaffection. He remarked naïvely that "he & all his brothers & sisters seceded from home in early life but they all returned. So would the States."[2] In early March, Lincoln said, "I can't afford to let Seward take the first trick."[3]

Seward believed that the Fort Sumter garrison should be withdrawn. To help persuade Lincoln to his way of thinking, he enlisted the aid of General Winfield Scott, the army's commanding general. The vain, rotund, elderly Scott had been a hard-liner in the fall of

1860, but during the winter, Seward cultivated him assiduously and won him over. So Scott recommended that Sumter be abandoned, much to Lincoln's astonishment.

The president seriously entertained Scott's proposal, for the general had great authority, and Lincoln, with no military background, may have been tempted to acquiesce. He could blame the necessity of surrendering Sumter on the Buchanan administration, which had dithered while the South Carolinians installed a ring of artillery around the fort. Moreover, on the Ides of March, the cabinet endorsed the general's suggestion, with only Montgomery Blair dissenting. But Lincoln did not accept the general's advice. Instead, he endorsed a plan concocted by Blair's brother-in-law Gustavus V. Fox, a former naval officer: troops and supplies would be conveyed to Charleston on a large commercial ship, then placed on swift tugboats that would whisk them to Sumter at night under the protective guns of a warship.

Meanwhile, the press touched off a firestorm of protest by reporting that Sumter would be surrendered to the South Carolinians. An Illinois Republican leader indignantly declared that "it is of no use (however true it may be) to tell *us*, we *can not* keep or retake the public property at the South ('hold, occupy, and possess'). We can try. We can shed our *treasure* and *blood* in the defence and support of our principles and *lawful rights* as our Fathers did." Thousands who had voted for Lincoln stood ready to "cheerfully shoulder their musket and hazard their *all* in *this world* in support of the principles for which we contended then. We have *compromised* and *truckled long* enough. War is bad. Civil war is worse, but if liberty and the right of the people to govern themselves was worth fighting for in the days of the Revolution, it is worth fighting for now."[4]

Lincoln feared that turning the fort over to South Carolina would not only be politically unpopular but also be tantamount to recognizing the legitimacy of secession. He further understood that reinforcing Sumter could touch off a war for which the North could be held responsible. A possible way out of this dilemma was to reinforce the only other major Deep South fort still in Union hands: Fort Pickens, off Pensacola, Florida. That gesture would demonstrate the administration's determination to hold its property; Sumter could then be abandoned on grounds of military necessity, for conditions there were exceptionally unfavorable for the government. So Lincoln ordered the reinforcement of Pickens and contemplated removing the Sumter garrison as soon as word arrived that the Florida fort had been reinforced.

The plan looked good in theory, but it did not work in practice. When the ships carrying reinforcements to Pickens arrived at their destination, the lieutenant in charge of the fort refused to accept them! With the approval of the Buchanan administration, he had made an informal agreement with the Florida authorities to receive no reinforcements if the Floridians would agree not to attack the fort. Exasperated by the failure of his plan, Lincoln on March 29 ordered the implementation Fox's scheme to resupply Fort Sumter.

Seward, who had been assuring Confederate emissaries that Sumter would be abandoned, panicked. On April 1, in a memorandum entitled "Some Thoughts for the President's Consideration," he brazenly suggested that he be allowed to take control of the administration and that the United States should go to war with Spain or France. His foreign policy proposal was no sudden impulse; a few weeks earlier, he had declared that if a European nation invaded the United States, "all the hills of South Carolina would pour forth their population for the rescue of New York."[5]

Lincoln replied tactfully to Seward's April 1 memorandum, reminding the secretary that the administration's domestic policy was spelled out in the inaugural: "to hold, occupy and possess the forts, and all other property and places belonging to the government, and to collect the duties on imports." Lincoln dismissed Seward's proposed declaration of war against European powers, remarking that Spain's meddling in Santo Domingo was trivial. He delicately rejected Seward's offer to assume the responsibilities of the presidency.

On April 6, the president sent a message to the governor of South Carolina informing him that ships would soon arrive at Charleston carrying food for the Sumter garrison; that if the relief vessels were not fired on, the Union fleet would hold its fire; but if the South Carolinians did attack, the Union would reinforce the garrison as well as resupply it. Lincoln cleverly placed the Confederates in a bind:

if they allowed Sumter to be resupplied, it would be embarrassing, but if they shelled the relief vessels, they would be attacking ships merely trying to bring food to starving men. The Confederates, there-fore, and not the Lincoln administration, would be responsible for firing the first shot.

On April 12, as Gustavus Fox's fleet was sailing toward Charleston, Confederate President Jefferson Davis ordered the bombardment of Sumter. He evidently thought that once war began, the Upper South and the Border States would join the Confederacy. As it turned out, four of those states did so (Virginia, Tennessee, Arkansas, and North Carolina), but four did not (Maryland, Kentucky, Delaware, and Missouri).

Lincoln has been criticized for cynically inveigling the South into beginning the war, but that is not just. He did not want war, but if war were to come, he wanted the South blamed for starting it. By sending supplies to Sumter, Lincoln realized that he might be precipitating hostilities, but that was not certain.

In a draft of Lincoln's July 4, 1861, message to Congress, he sum-marized the reasoning behind his decision: "I believed . . . that to [withdraw the Sumter garrison] . . . would be utterly ruinous—that the *necessity* under which it was to be done, would not be fully under-stood—that, by many, it would be construed as a part of a *voluntary* policy—that, at home, it would discourage the friends of the Union, embolden it's foes, and insure to the latter a recognition abroad—that, in fact, it would be our national destruction consummated."[6]

Demonstrating masterful leadership, Lincoln had kept Seward from taking the first trick, and he had not allowed the Confederates to corner him. Weeks later, Seward told his wife: "Executive skill and vigor are rare qualities. The President is the best of us."[7]

In March 1865, Lincoln succinctly analyzed the outbreak of hos-tilities: "Both parties deprecated war, but one of them would *make* war rather than let the nation survive, and the other would *accept* war rather than let it perish, and the war came."[8] Lincoln was willing to accept war because, as he told a friend, "far less evil & bloodshed would result from an effort to maintain the Union and the Constitu-tion, than from disruption and the formation of two confederacies."[9]

THE WAR BEGINS

I n the days immediately after the attack on Fort Sumter, Lincoln faced daunting challenges. He later described the situation: the war "began on very unequal terms between the parties. The insurgents had been preparing for it more than thirty years, while the government had taken no steps to resist them. The former had carefully considered all the means which could be turned to their account. It undoubtedly was a well pondered reliance with them that in their own unrestricted effort to destroy Union, constitution, and law, all together, the government would, in great degree, be restrained by the same constitution and law, from arresting their progress. Their sympathizers pervaded all departments of the government, and nearly all communities of the people."[1]

During the first hundred days of the war, Lincoln showed the "indomitable will" that he had once attributed to Henry Clay.[2] He raised, supplied, and sent into battle a vastly increased army; kept the Border States within the Union; helped stymie Confederate efforts to gain diplomatic recognition; established a blockade; took effective charge of his cabinet; skillfully managed Congress; avoided giving offense to Great Britain; and eloquently explained the nature and purpose of the war. In accomplishing these ends, Lincoln managed to be forceful without being obstinate or autocratic and somehow infused his own iron will into his constituents as they fought to save what he called "the last, best hope of earth."[3]

On Friday, April 12, when news of the bombardment of Sumter reached him, Lincoln calmly observed that "he did not expect it so soon," for he anticipated that the South Carolinians would not begin shelling the fort before the fleet arrived.[4] That day, Lincoln met with an official who wrote that the president "is as firm as a rock, & means to show the world that there is a United States of America left yet."[5] On Sunday, Lincoln and the cabinet composed a proclamation calling out the militia, basing it on the 1795 Militia Act. Some recommended that fifty thousand men be summoned; others suggested twice as many. Lincoln decided to compromise on the number, asking for seventy-five thousand men for three months' service. When it was argued that the North had superior resolve and enterprise, Lincoln observed, "We must not forget that the people of the seceded States, like those of the loyal ones, are American citizens, with essentially the same characteristics and powers. Exceptional advantages on one side are counterbalanced by exceptional advantages on the other. We must make up our minds that man for man the soldier from the South will be a match for the soldier from the North and *vice versa*."[6]

Lincoln's anger at secessionist leaders shone through the language of the proclamation. In drafting that document, he alluded to "[in] sults, and injuries already too long endured." Explaining the appeal to arms, he stressed an argument that he would repeatedly make during the war: "I appeal to all loyal citizens to favor, facilitate, and aid this effort to maintain the honor, the integrity, and the existence of our National Union and the perpetuity of popular government." The aim of the conflict was to vindicate democracy. The immediate goal of the troops, he stated, would "probably be to repossess the forts, places and property, which have been seized from the Union."[7]

That language was unfortunate, for it drove North Carolina, Virginia, Arkansas, and Tennessee into the arms of the Confederacy. If Lincoln had appealed for troops to protect Washington, D.C., from invasion, Unionists in those four states would have been strengthened; as it was, they were fatally weakened. In Virginia, William C. Rives denounced "Mr. Lincoln's unlucky & ill-conceived proclamation," saying that it caused the Old Dominion to secede. "Before that, all the proceedings of the Convention indicated an earnest desire to maintain the Union," Rives asserted.[8]

Lincoln soon realized his mistake. On April 21, he told the mayor of Baltimore, "I am not a learned man!" and maintained "that his proclamation had not been correctly understood; that he had no intention of bringing on war, but that his purpose was to defend the capital, which was in danger of being bombarded from the heights across the Potomac."⁹ Repeatedly he "protested, on his honor, in the most solemn way, that the troops were meant exclusively to protect the Capital."¹⁰

Other critics faulted Lincoln for calling up too few men. Horace Greeley insisted that five hundred thousand militia should have been enlisted. But that number was not realistic. The regular army was only seventeen thousand strong, and the North's arsenals as well as the U.S. treasury were virtually empty. Moreover, the 1795 Militia Act stipulated that the men who were called up could serve for only thirty days after the next session of Congress began.

Most Northerners reacted to the proclamation enthusiastically. As Lincoln later stated, "the response of the country was most gratifying to the administration, surpassing, in unanimity and spirit, the most sanguine expectation."¹¹ A Vermonter reported that people in his state "have felt for the last three months mortified, indignant, 'mad clear through' at the disgrace & shame inflicted on us & we now rejoice & are glad that the insults heaped on us are to be avenged, & our wounded honor vindicated."¹² Wisconsin Senator James R. Doolittle observed that if "an Angel from Heaven had issued a proclamation it could hardly have received a heartier response than the proclamation of the President."¹³

As thousands of men rushed to the recruiting stations, the administration faced a serious question: should Congress be called immediately into special session to help deal with the crisis? Lincoln hesitated because several states had not elected representatives and were therefore unrepresented in the new House, which was scheduled to convene in December. (In that era, not all states held elections for Congress in November of even-numbered years.) Moreover, it was not clear that congressmen and senators could safely assemble in Washington, which was nestled between two slave states (Maryland and Virginia). Lincoln therefore decided not to summon Congress into session right away but to delay the opening until July 4. But meantime, emergency steps had to be taken. And so Lincoln spent unappropriated money, expanded the regular army, blockaded Southern ports, and authorized the suspension of the writ of habeas corpus, all without congressional approval. Acting decisively, he assumed that Congress would retroactively approve his action, which it did that summer. On July 1, Lincoln told a senator "that he did not know of any law to authorize some things which he had done; but he thought there was a necessity for them, & that to save the constitution & the laws generally, it might be better to do some illegal acts, rather than suffer all to be overthrown."[14]

A year later, the president explained that there "was no adequate and effective organization for the public defence. Congress had indefinitely adjourned. There was no time to convene them. It became necessary for me to choose whether, using only the existing means, agencies, and processes which Congress had provided, I should let the government fall at once into ruin, or whether, availing myself of the broader powers conferred by the Constitution in cases of insurrection, I would make an effort to save it with all its blessings for the present age and for posterity. . . . I believe that by these and other similar measures taken in that crisis, some of which were without any authority of law, the government was saved from overthrow."[15]

Some Democrats complained that the president had "two months of absolute despotic control."[16] Subsequent critics have echoed that charge, but it is difficult to fault Lincoln's decision, made as it was amid the uncertain conditions immediately following the attack on Fort Sumter.

Those conditions were unsettling indeed. On April 17, Virginia seceded; the next day, Union troops abandoned Harpers Ferry after setting the armory there afire; on the twentieth, Union forces also burned the Gosport Navy Yard at Norfolk before leaving it. Washingtonians, doubtful of the loyalty of the local militia, feared that their city would be seized. Anxiously they anticipated the arrival of Northern troops. On April 20, a member of the Frontier Guards, an informal military unit hastily assembled to defend the capital, wrote in his diary: "A universal gloom and anxiety sits upon every

countenance." The city was "rife with treason, and the street full of
traitors." Plaintively he asked, "[W]hen will reinforcements come?
Will it be too late?"[17]

Day after day passed with no sign of Northern troops, prompting
Lincoln to exclaim: "Why don't they come! Why don't they come!"[18]
Adding to his anxiety, approximately one-third of the officers in the
army and navy resigned, including Colonel Robert E. Lee, who on
April 23 took command of the military forces of his native Virginia.
Had Lee decided to remain true to his oath and support the govern-
ment that educated and paid him, the Civil War would doubtless
have been much shorter and far less bloody.

On April 18, five unarmed companies of Pennsylvania militiamen
arrived in Washington, relieving tension somewhat. The following
day, a Baltimore mob attacked the Massachusetts Sixth Regiment
as it passed through the city en route to Washington. Four soldiers
were killed and thirty-six wounded. Upon their arrival in the capital,
Lincoln told the colonel in charge, "Thank God, you have come;
for if you had not Washington would have been in the hands of the
rebels before morning. Your brave boys have saved the capital. God
bless them."[19]

On April 20, to prevent further outbreaks of street violence, Maryland officials issued orders to destroy all bridges on rail lines linking
Baltimore with the rest of the North. Communication with the capital ceased when telegraph wires were also cut and mail service was
halted. Troops bound for Washington wasted days seeking alternate
routes. Lincoln later declared that a man "who strangles himself, for
whatever motive, is not more unreasonable than were those citizens
of Baltimore who, in a single night, destroyed the Baltimore and
Ohio railroad, the Northern Central railroad, and the railroad from
Baltimore to Philadelphia."[20]

At the urging of Maryland officials, Lincoln, fearing that more
bloody clashes in Baltimore might drive the Free State out of the
Union, ordered troops to pass around rather than through that city,
which was known as "Mobtown." On April 22, other Baltimore
residents insisted that no troops be allowed to pass through any part
of Maryland. Angered by this new demand, Lincoln scolded them:

"You, gentlemen, come here to me and ask for peace on any terms, and yet have no word of condemnation for those who are making war on us. You express great horror of bloodshed, and yet would not lay a straw in the way of those who are organizing in Virginia and elsewhere to capture this city. The rebels attack Fort Sumter, and your citizens attack troops sent to the defense of the Government, and the lives and property in Washington, and yet you would have me break my oath and surrender the Government without a blow. There is no Washington in that—no Jackson in that—no manhood nor honor in that." Lincoln added that he had "no desire to invade the South; but I must have the troops, and mathematically the necessity exists that they should come through Maryland. They can't crawl under the earth, and they can't fly over it. Why, sir, those Carolinians are now crossing Virginia to come here to hang me, and what can I do?"[21] Northerners united in declaring that if troops were not allowed to pass through Baltimore, the "city and its name should be swept from the face of the earth."[22] On April 27, Lincoln explained that "he could easily have destroyed Baltimore, but that it would have been visiting vengeance upon a large body of loyal citizens, who were the property-holders, for the sake of punishing the mob who had committed the outrage upon the Massachusetts troops, but which mob, as to property, had little or nothing to lose."[23]

On April 24, gloom settled over Washington like a toxic cloud. Despairing, Lincoln told members of the Massachusetts Sixth, "I don't believe there is any North. The Seventh [New York] Regiment is a myth. R[hode] Island is not known in our geography any longer. *You* are the only Northern realities."[24]

The following day, the gloomy cloud lifted as the New York Seventh Regiment reached Washington, making Lincoln "the happiest-looking man in town."[25] Other units arrived soon thereafter, assuring the safety of the capital. Lincoln's order to route troops around rather than through Baltimore helped Maryland Unionists triumph over their foes in elections that June and November.

In July, Lincoln submitted to the freshly assembled Congress a message explaining his unusual conduct over the preceding weeks. His most controversial step had been authorizing General Winfield

Scott to suspend the writ of habeas corpus, thus permitting the army to detain people without charges. Alluding to some arrests made in the capital, Lincoln urged Scott to use that power sparingly: "Unless the *necessity* for . . . arbitrary arrests is *manifest*, and *urgent*, I prefer that they should cease."[26]

In May, the octogenarian chief justice of the U.S. Supreme Court, Roger B. Taney, challenged the administration's suspension of the privilege of the writ of habeas corpus. John Merryman, a prosecession Marylander who had helped disrupt communications between Washington and the North, was detained for allegedly training men for service in the Confederate army. Taney, sitting as a circuit court of appeals judge, ruled that the Constitution authorized Congress, not the president, to suspend the writ of habeas corpus. Lincoln disregarded Taney's order to release Merryman, who remained a prisoner for weeks.

Lincoln rejected Taney's argument. In a draft version of his July 4 message to Congress, he laid out his counterargument: "The whole of the laws which I was sworn to take care that they be faithfully executed, were being resisted, and failing to be executed, in nearly one third of the states. Must I have allowed them to finally fail of execution, even had it been perfectly clear that by the use of the means necessary to their execution, some single law, made in such extreme tenderness of the citizens liberty, that practically, it relieves more of the guilty, than the innocent, should, to a very limited extent, be violated? To state the question more directly, are all the laws, but one, to go unexecuted, and the government itself go to pieces, lest that one be violated? Even in such a case I should consider my official oath broken if I should allow the government to be overthrown, when I might think that disregarding the single law would tend to preserve it—But, in this case I was not, in my own judgment, driven to this ground—In my opinion I violated no law—The provision of the Constitution that 'The previlege of the writ of habeas corpus, shall not be suspended unless when, in cases of rebellion or invasion, the public safety may require it' is equivalent to a provision—is a provision—that such previlege may be suspended when, in cases of rebellion, or invasion, the public safety does require it. I decided that we have a case of rebellion, and that the public safety does require the qualified suspension of the previlege of the writ of habeas corpus, which I authorized to be made. Now it is insisted that Congress, and not the executive, is vested with this power—But the Constitution itself, is silent as to which, or who, is to exercise the power; and as the provision plainly was made for a dangerous emergency, I can not bring myself to believe that the framers of that instrument intended that in every case the danger should run it's course until Congress could be called together, the very assembling of which might be prevented, as was intended in this case, by the rebellion."[27]

Lincoln had a good case: in those days. Congress was typically out of session more than half the year, during which time foreign invaders might attack or insurrectionaries might rebel and make it impossible for Congress to assemble (as they had done in April).

Taney had maintained that since the suspension clause of the Constitution appears in Article I, which deals primarily with the powers of Congress, that body and not the president had the power to suspend the writ. But the chief justice did not acknowledge that the original draft of the suspension clause read: "the privileges and benefit of the Writ of Habeas Corpus shall be enjoyed in this Government in the most expeditious and ample manner; and shall not be suspended by the Legislature except upon the most urgent and pressing occasions, and for a limited time not exceeding _____ months." Gouverneur Morris later moved to revise that language to read as it does in the final version. By dropping the phrase "by the Legislature," the framers implied that Congress was not the only branch of government authorized to suspend the writ.[28]

In 1862, a federal circuit court ruled in *ex parte Field* that the 1795 Militia Act, authorizing the president to suppress rebellions, implicitly granted him the power to suspend habeas corpus. Decades later, the U.S. Supreme Court in *Moyer v. Peabody* (1909) endorsed the Circuit Court's ruling in *ex parte Field*. Thus it is reasonable to conclude that Lincoln acted within the Constitution by suspending habeas corpus when a serious insurrection was underway (and as long as Congress did not prohibit him from doing so).

Throughout the war, Lincoln exercised restraint in dealing with civil liberties, especially compared with other wartime presidents (e.g., John Adams during the quasi-war with France, Woodrow Wilson during World War I, and Franklin D. Roosevelt during World War II). Political opponents roundly criticized his administration; newspapers were rarely censored, even when they recommended that the president be assassinated; free and fair elections were conducted regularly, with some exceptions in the Border States; courts remained open; and legislatures assembled without federal hindrance (with one brief exception). Democrats nonetheless protested against the "irresponsible despotism of Abraham Lincoln!"[29]

In the early stages of the war, Lincoln struggled mightily to keep the Border States, especially Kentucky, from seceding. "I think to lose Kentucky, is nearly the same as to lose the whole game," he told a friend. "Kentucky gone, we can not hold Missouri, nor as I think, Maryland. These all against us, and the job on our hands is too large for us. We would as well consent to separation at once, including the surrender of the capital."[30] Kentucky's large population, its strategic location, and its valuable resources made the Bluegrass State exceptionally important. To avoid driving it into the arms of the Confederacy, Lincoln tactfully soft-pedaled the slavery issue and reluctantly honored the state's initial desire to remain neutral in the war. To those who recommended that he dispatch troops to defend persecuted Kentucky Unionists, Lincoln responded, "I am exceedingly anxious to protect the Union men, and have taken all proper measures to do so, as well in Kentucky as in Tennessee, but I am the head of a great nation, and must be governed by wide forethought, as far as possible. I will illustrate my position by the fable of the farmer who returned home and found that, while his two little children were asleep, a number of snakes had taken part possession of the bed. He could not strike the snakes without endangering his offspring, and, therefore, he had to stay his hand."[31] But, he added, "I do not want to act in a hurry about this matter; I don't want to hurt anybody in Kentucky, but I will get the serpent out of Tennessee."[32]

Though he did not send forces into Kentucky, Lincoln worked behind the scenes to strengthen the hand of Unionists there. He authorized William "Bull" Nelson, a navy lieutenant on loan to the army, and Major Robert Anderson, a native of the Bluegrass State and the hero of Fort Sumter, to recruit troops in western Virginia and Kentucky. To lead those troops, Lincoln detailed able officers to Kentucky. In addition, the president had weapons smuggled into the state (among them, twenty thousand rifles, known as "Lincoln guns"). Lincoln's tactful handling of Kentucky paid handsome dividends at the polls. In June, Unionists won nine of the state's ten congressional seats; in August, they captured 103 of the 138 General Assembly seats.

On September 3, Confederate General Leonidas Polk ended Kentucky's neutrality when he rashly occupied Columbus, whereupon Union troops under Ulysses S. Grant seized Paducah. The state legislature demanded that Polk's troops withdraw but not Grant's. The Confederates' blunder helped solidify Kentucky's loyalty to the Union.

Keeping Missouri loyal posed especially difficult challenges. Its governor, the prosecession Claiborne F. Jackson, hoped to seize the St. Louis arsenal and turn all its weapons and ammunition over to the Confederates. An impulsive Union captain, Nathaniel Lyon, however, captured the governor's prosecessionist militia and foiled Jackson's scheme.

Lyon's bold move did not please Lincoln, who wanted to proceed cautiously in Missouri. He told a Missouri officeholder that "if he was compelled to send men from one side of Missouri to the other[,] which he did not anticipate[,] he would rather send them around than through the State in order to avoid any trouble. No troops will be sent to Missouri from other States. In short everything tending to arouse the jealousy of the people will be avoided."[33]

At the urging of Congressman Frank Blair, the leading Unionist in Missouri, Lincoln overcame his own misgivings and placed Lyon in charge of Union forces in the state. In August, Lyon impetuously attacked a superior enemy force at Wilson's Creek, where his troops were repulsed, and he was killed. Seven months later, however, at the battle of Pea Ridge, Arkansas, Union forces defeated the Rebels, effectively ending formal armed resistance to federal authority in Missouri. Thereafter, informal guerilla warfare and savage bushwhacking prevailed in that troubled state. Missouri nevertheless remained loyal to the Union.

While striving to retain the loyal Border States in the Union, Lincoln did not ignore foreign affairs. Britain and France, he knew, were eager to keep their textile mills busy with cotton from the South. To prevent those nations from intervening on behalf of the Confederacy, Lincoln exercised the utmost tact in dealing with them.

A crisis developed shortly after the war began. In response to Lincoln's declaration of intention to declare a blockade, the British government issued a Proclamation of Neutrality, which seemed to many outraged Northerners like a prelude to diplomatic recognition. Officially, though, it gave the Confederacy only belligerent status. Prime Minister Palmerston, eager to avoid entanglement in the American war, thought it best to declare neutrality as a reply to the Lincoln administration's planned blockade.

Secretary of State Seward publicly protested to the British minister, Lord Lyons, and privately cursed the Palmerston ministry: "God damn them, I'll give them hell."[34] He was mad not only at the proclamation but also at the British government's willingness to meet informally with Confederate emissaries. Seward drafted a heated protest to be submitted by the American minister in London, Charles Francis Adams, to her majesty's government. Lincoln toned it down significantly, substituting "The President regrets" for "The President is surprised and grieved"; "Such intercourse would be none the less hurtful to us" instead of "Such intercourse would be none the less wrongful to us"; "No one of these proceedings will pass unnoticed by the United States" instead of "No one of these proceedings will be borne by the United States." Lincoln also suggested that Adams be told: "This paper is for your own guidance only, and not be read, or shown to any one." This sentence replaced the intemperate final passage in Seward's draft instructions.[35] Thus Lincoln helped defuse what could have been a diplomatic crisis leading to war with Great Britain.

Though the administration had little trouble recruiting troops in the wake of the attack on Fort Sumter, supplying, equipping, feeding, and training them proved an overwhelming challenge for the inept Secretary of War Simon Cameron and his hapless bureau chiefs. The department, like much of the rest of the nation, was ill-prepared to organize large-scale enterprises. The small, elderly staff suffered from bureaucratic sclerosis, and Cameron was preoccupied with awarding contracts to political friends rather than mobilizing the North for warfare on a far vaster scale than the Mexican War or the War of 1812. The hero of those conflicts, the septuagenarian, obese, and gout-ridden General Winfield Scott, was well past his prime. Compounding matters, Cameron's agents, including his henchman Alexander Cummings, paid exorbitant sums for inferior equipment, weapons, shoes, and uniforms. Corrupt quartermasters defrauded the government of millions of dollars.

Several weeks into the war, Lincoln admitted that his administration had "stumbled along," but he thought that, all things considered, it had done so "in the right direction."[36] He made some blunders, partly because he was so preoccupied with the distribution of both civilian and military patronage.

Offsetting the weakness of the war department were the efficiency of Quartermaster General Montgomery Meigs (appointed over Cameron's objections); the organizational savvy of Assistant Secretary of War Thomas A. Scott, on loan to the government from the Pennsylvania Railroad; Edward S. Sanford, president of the American Telegraph Company, who took charge of military telegraphs; the resourcefulness of civilian volunteer organizations like the U.S. Sanitary Commission (founded to help promote the health and welfare of the army), the New York Defence Committee, and the volunteer nursing corps headed by the redoubtable Dorothea Dix; and the energetic efforts of some unusually capable Northern governors (especially in Massachusetts, New York, Indiana, and Pennsylvania).

When those governors complained about the administration's failure to supply their wants quickly, Lincoln assured them that he and his aides "are doing the very best we can." To Oliver P. Morton of Indiana (whom Lincoln called "a good fellow, but at times . . . the skeerdest man I know of"), he wrote, "You do not receive arms from us as fast as you need them; but it is because we have not near enough to meet all the pressing demands; and we are obliged to share around what we have, sending the larger share to the points which appear to need them most. We have great hope that our own supply will be ample before long, so that you and all others can have as many as you need."[37] When Governor Edwin D. Morgan of New York protested that confusion reigned in the war department, Lincoln replied, "The enthusiastic uprising of the people in our cause, is our great reliance; and we can not safely give it any check, even though it overflows, and runs in channels not laid down in any chart."[38]

When Congress assembled on July 4, Lincoln submitted to it one of his ablest state papers, a special message in which he reviewed his actions since the outbreak of hostilities and explained his understanding of the stakes involved in the war.

In his dealings with Congress, Lincoln was courteous and tactful, but he did not follow the Whig doctrine that the president should defer to the legislature and merely carry out its wishes as expressed in laws. To be sure, though he now and then paid lip service to that doctrine, he was in fact an assertive chief executive, unafraid to make difficult decisions and unintimidated by senators, congressman, governors, generals, editors, cabinet members, or anyone else.

Lincoln's manner was far from autocratic, however. He had an innate modesty that endeared him to many Northerners. A Missourian who watched him receive visitors reported that he displayed "no airs of assumed or hereditary dignity, nor stiffness, nor carrying the importance of the Presidential office into every day acts. His reception of men is cordial and unaffected, and his manner devoid of any personal claim for respect from the office he holds." His appearance on the streets of the capital won the public's favor. The "half jaunty air . . . of his hat, as he rides in his barouche, beside Mrs. Lincoln, of an evening, is consoling to the spectator, who instinctively feels that even if he can write State papers with original and trenchant ability, yet a man of easy manners and kind good nature is Mr. President."[39]

In his message, Lincoln placed the war in world historical perspective: "Our popular government, has often been called an experiment. Two points in it our people have already settled—the successful *establishing* and the successful *administering* of it. One still remains—it's successful *maintenance* against a formidable attempt to overthrow it. It is now for them to demonstrate to the world, that those who can fairly carry an election, can also suppress a rebellion; that ballots are the rightful, and peaceful, successors of bullets; and that when ballots have fairly, and constitutionally decided, there can be no successful appeal back to bullets; that there can be no successful appeal, except to ballots themselves, at succeeding elections. Such will be a great lesson of peace; teaching men that what they cannot take by an election, neither can they take it by a war; teaching all, the folly of being the beginners of a war." He foreshadowed the famous speech he would give at Gettysburg in 1863: "And this issue embraces more than the fate of these United States. It presents to the whole family of man the question, whether a Constitutional republic, or a democracy—a government of the people, by the same people—can, or cannot, maintain its territorial integrity against its own domestic foes. It presents the question, whether discontented individuals, too few in numbers to control administration, according to organic law, in any case, can always, upon the pretences made in this case, or on any other pretences, or arbitrarily, without any pretence, break up their government, and thus practically put an end to free government upon the earth. It forces us to ask: 'Is there, in all republics, this inherent and fatal weakness?' 'Must a government, of necessity, be too strong for the liberties of its own people, or too *weak* to maintain its own existence?'"[40]

Lincoln called the war "essentially a People's contest." For Unionists, "it is a struggle for maintaining in the world, that form and substance of government, whose leading object is, to elevate the condition of men—to lift artificial weights from all shoulders; to clear the paths of laudable pursuit for all; to afford all, an unfettered start, and a fair chance, in the race of life. Yielding to partial and temporary departures, from necessity, this is the leading object of the government for whose existence we contend." There were, he said, "many single regiments whose members, one and another, possess full practical knowledge of all the arts, sciences, professions, and whatever else, whether useful or elegant, is known in the world; and there is scarcely one, from which there could not be selected, a President, a Cabinet, a Congress, and perhaps a Court, abundantly competent to administer the government itself."[41]

Lincoln reviewed the lead-up to war, explaining the decision to relieve Fort Sumter and offering yet again a refutation of the secessionists' "ingenious sophism" that "any State of the Union may, *consistently* with the national Constitution, and therefore *lawfully*, and *peacefully*, withdraw from the Union, without the consent of the Union, or of any other State. The little disguise that the supposed right is to be exercised only for just cause, themselves to be the sole judge of its justice, is too thin to merit any notice. With rebellion thus sugar-coated, they have been drugging the public mind of their section for more than thirty years; and, until at length, they have brought many good men to a willingness to take up arms against the government the day after some assemblage of men have enacted the farcical pretence of taking their State out of the Union, who could have been brought to no such thing the day *before*."[42]

Lincoln argued that if he had let Southern states pull out of the Union, he would have set a dangerous precedent: "by allowing the seceders to go in peace, it is difficult to see what we can do, if others choose to go, or to extort terms upon which they will promise to remain."[43]

Lincoln requested Congress to endorse the steps he had taken in the ten weeks since the fall of Fort Sumter: "It was with the deepest regret that the Executive found the duty of employing the war-power, in defence of the government, forced upon him. He could but perform this duty, or surrender the existence of the government. No compromise, by public servants, could, in this case, be a cure; not that compromises are not often proper, but that no popular government can long survive a marked precedent, that those who carry an election, can only save the government from immediate destruction, by giving up the main point, upon which the people gave the election. The people themselves, and not their servants, can safely reverse their own deliberate decisions. As a private citizen, the Executive could not have consented that these institutions shall perish; much less could he, in betrayal of so vast, and so sacred a trust, as these free people had confided to him. He felt that he had no moral right to shrink; nor even to count the chances of his own life, in what might follow. In full view of his great responsibility, he has, so far, done what he has deemed his duty. You will now, according to your own judgment, perform yours."[44]

Lincoln endorsed the creation of an immense army and the appropriation of astronomical sums of money: "It is now recommended that you give the legal means for making this contest a short, and a decisive one; that you place at the control of the government, for the work, at least four hundred thousand men, and four hundred millions of dollars."[45]

The public generally approved of the message. The editor of *Harper's Weekly* deemed it "the most truly American message ever delivered. Think upon what a millennial year we have fallen when the President of the United States declares officially that this government is founded upon the rights of man! Wonderfully acute, simple, sagacious, and of antique honesty! I can forgive the jokes and the big hands, and the inability to make bows. Some of us who doubted were wrong."[46] In Lincoln's hometown, the Republican *Illinois State Journal* was pleased that the message contained "no 'niggerism'" (that is, no mention of slavery), but Frederick Douglass was not: "Any one reading that document, with no previous knowledge of the United States, would never dream from any thing there written that we have a slaveholders war waged upon the Government."[47]

Congress retroactively approved all of Lincoln's emergency measures except the suspension of habeas corpus. (It waited until March 1863 to ratify that action.) In 1863, the U.S. Supreme Court in the *Prize Cases* followed suit, ruling that the president's declaration of a blockade without congressional authorization was constitutional.

In late July, Congress approved a resolution asserting that the war was not being waged "in any spirit of oppression, or for any purpose of conquest or subjugation, or purpose of overthrowing or interfering with the rights or established institutions" of the seceding states. But Congress did pass legislation authorizing the seizure of any property, including slaves, used in direct support of Confederate military operations. Lincoln was unenthusiastic about this so-called Confiscation Act, which he believed might violate the Constitution's Fifth Amendment (which stipulated that the government could not seize property without just compensation) as well as its provision that "no attainder of treason shall work corruption of blood, or forfeiture, except during the life of the person attainted." Reluctantly, he did sign the measure, but he did little to enforce it.

Meanwhile, Lincoln laid plans for a military offensive. "I intend to give *blows*," he remarked a week after the fall of Sumter. "The only question at present is, whether I should first retake Fort Sumter or Harpers Ferry."[48] The general-in-chief, Winfield Scott, had other ideas, proposing a so-called Anaconda Plan to crush the rebellion with a blockade and a "powerful movement down the Mississippi." But this scheme seemed too passive for impatient Northerners like Horace Greeley, whose *New York Tribune* demanded, "Forward to Richmond! Forward to Richmond!" The Confederate Congress should be prevented from meeting in the Virginia capital on July 20 as planned, insisted the *Tribune*: "By that date the place must be held by the national army!"[49]

Lincoln, too, grew impatient, and so he rejected the Anaconda Plan. Figuring that fifty thousand Union troops in northern Virginia could defeat thirty thousand Confederate troops there, he authorized an offensive devised by General Irvin McDowell, calling for an attack on P. G. T. Beauregard's army near Manassas, thirty miles southwest of Washington. In addition, the president realized that the ninety-day enlistment of many Federal troops would soon expire, and he wanted to provide them with "a chance to smell powder before discharging them from service."[50] When told that the Union troops required more training, Lincoln noted that the Confederates did, too: "You are green, it is true; but they are green, also; you are all green alike."[51]

McDowell's plan seemed promising but only if Confederates under Joseph E. Johnston in the Shenandoah Valley were unable to link up with Beauregard. The seventeen thousand Union troops under General Robert Patterson were to keep Johnston preoccupied while McDowell attacked Beauregard.

On July 21, McDowell's troops crossed Bull Run and drove the Confederates back so easily that it seemed as if victory was inevitable. But Johnston evaded Patterson and reinforced Beauregard and thus helped the Confederates drive McDowell's men from the field.

At first, Lincoln received news of the defeat calmly, but when the extent of the rout became clear, he said with intense emotion, "[I]f Hell is [not] any worse than this, it has no terror for me."[52] He refused, however, to be discouraged. A few days after the battle, he said, "We were all too confident—too sure of an easy victory. We now understand the difficulties in the way, and shall surmount them."[53]

Promptly, Lincoln came up with a new strategy: rapid implementation of a blockade; more training of troops at Fort Monroe; retaining Baltimore "with a gentle, but firm, and certain hand"; increasing forces in the Shenandoah Valley; making Missouri a higher priority; reorganizing veterans of the Manassas campaign; discharging all ninety-day enlistees unwilling to serve longer; and deploying new volunteers along the Potomac. Then Union forces were to move against Memphis, East Tennessee, Virginia's Shenandoah Valley, and Manassas.[54]

To implement this strategy, Lincoln recalled General George B. McClellan from western Virginia, where he enjoyed success against Confederate forces. Since he was the only Union general who had done so, McClellan seemed the obvious choice to replace McDowell. Prominent officers assured Lincoln that McClellan "possessed a very high order of military talent," and the president "did not think they could all be mistaken."[55]

On July 27, when McClellan took charge of the Division of the Potomac, Northern morale soared. Little Mac would transform the demoralized army and lead it to victory, thus ending the war. Or so it was thought.

STALEMATE

Between August 1861 and March 1862, newspapers ran many stories headlined: "all quiet on the Potomac." Initially, that was an accurate description of the military situation in the East; in time, "all quiet on the Potomac" became something more, a derisive commentary on McClellan's timidity.

In December 1861, Lincoln explained why the Union army had made no advance since the Bull Run debacle: "If I were sure of victory we would have one at once, but we cannot stand a defeat, & we must be certain of victory before we strike."[1] McClellan, who shared that opinion, refused to send the army forward, even though he had trained and equipped it magnificently soon after he took command. As a result, for six months the conflict was little more than a sitzkrieg (sitting war) instead of a blitzkrieg (lightning war).

Lincoln patiently tolerated the inactivity of the thirty-four-year-old McClellan, who viewed himself as a savior. Soon after arriving in Washington, the general wrote his wife, "I find myself in a new & strange position here—Presdt, Cabinet, Genl Scott & all deferring to me—by some strange operation of magic I seem to have become the power of the land. I almost think that were I to win some small success now I could become Dictator or anything else that might please me—but nothing of that kind would please me—*therefore* I *won't* be Dictator. Admirable self denial!" Without evident irony, he added, "I am not spoiled by my unexpected & new position—I feel sure that God will give me the strength & wisdom to preserve this great nation. . . . I feel that God has placed a great work in my hands."[2]

In his career, the general had known nothing but success. He had ranked second in his West Point class, had served with distinction in the Mexican War, had led a group to observe the Crimean War, had devised a cavalry saddle, had assumed the presidency of a railroad after leaving the army in 1857, had commanded Ohio's militia at the war's start, had become a major general in the regular army in May 1861, and had led the only Union forces that won victories early in the war.

While the North rejoiced at McClellan's success in western Virginia, the general had shown there some unfortunate qualities, taking credit that was actually due others, chastising his subordinates unjustly, demonstrating indecisiveness and irresolution, failing to follow up on his victories, making promises that he did not honor, and whining unjustly about a lack of support.

On August 2, McClellan submitted an impractical plan that he claimed would allow him to "carry this thing on 'En grand' & crush the rebels in one campaign."[3] Inadequate as he might be as a strategist, he was exceptionally gifted as an organizer and administrator. He transformed the demoralized army into a disciplined, well-equipped fighting force that he renamed the Army of the Potomac. Because he exuded self-confidence, competence, and charm and because he appeared to care passionately about the troops' well-being, they admired him extravagantly.

Intensely ambitious, McClellan defiantly worked behind the scenes to undermine the general-in-chief of the army, Winfield Scott, whose job he coveted. Little Mac told his wife, "I do not know whether Scott is a dotard or a traitor! I can't tell which. He cannot or will not comprehend the condition in which we are placed & is entirely unequal to the emergency. If he cannot be taken out of my path I will not retain my position, but will resign & let the adm[instratio]n take care of itself." Scott "understands nothing, appreciates nothing & is ever in my way."[4] Ironically, McClellan denounced Scott as a man of "inaction" who was always on "the defensive."[5] Understandably, Scott took offense and refused to step aside.

For several weeks, Lincoln unsuccessfully attempted to paper over the differences between Scott and McClellan but ultimately concluded that Scott was too ill and too old to be effective. On November 1, Scott resigned, and McClellan took his place. Lincoln told the new general-in-chief, "I should be perfectly satisfied if I thought that this vast increase of responsibility would not embarrass you. Draw on me for all the sense I have, and all the information. In addition to your present command, the supreme command of the army will entail a vast labor upon you."

"I can do it all," McClellan said confidently.[6]

Northerners expected great things from Little Mac, for it was assumed that only Scott had kept him from advancing. But McClellan blamed the president even more emphatically than Scott for his troubles. He called Lincoln "an idiot," "the original gorilla," a "baboon," and "'an old stick'—& pretty poor timber at that." He criticized "the cowardice of the Presdt" and insisted that "I can never regard him with feeling other than those of thorough contempt—for his mind, heart & morality."[7]

McClellan's contempt for Lincoln, which was rooted in part in social snobbery, led him to treat the president shabbily. One night soon after becoming supreme commander, Little Mac returned to his house, where he found the president, John Hay, and Secretary of State Seward awaiting him. Hay noted in his diary that McClellan, "without paying any particular attention to the porter who told him the President was waiting to see him, went up stairs, passing the door of the room where the President and Secretary of State were seated. They waited about half-an-hour, and sent once more a servant to tell the General they were there, and the answer came that the General had gone to bed." En route back to the White House, Hay condemned "this unparalleled insolence of epaulettes," but Lincoln "seemed not to have noticed it specially, saying it was better at this time not to be making points of etiquette & personal dignity."[8] Time and again, McClellan snubbed the president, who magnanimously remarked, "Never mind; I will hold McClellan's horse if he will only bring us success."[9]

McClellan viewed other government leaders with contempt. He called the cabinet "a most despicable set of men." Seward in his view was "a meddling, officious, incompetent little puppy," Gideon Welles was "weaker than the most garrulous old woman you were ever annoyed by," and Edward Bates was an "inoffensive old man."[10] He also held congressional Radicals in contempt for their ideology as well as their meddlesome ways. A partisan Democrat with no sympathy for abolitionism or blacks, he acknowledged that he had "a prejudice in favor of my own race" and that he could not "learn to like the odor of either Billy goats or niggers." He told his wife, "I will not fight for the abolitionists."[11]

As time passed, it seemed to many Northerners that McClellan would not fight at all. In part, his timidity resulted from his chronic overestimation of the enemy's strength. He feared that the Confederates at Manassas had over 150,000 troops, far outnumbering his own forces. But in reality, he had between 85,000 and 100,000 effectives while his counterpart had only 30,000 to 35,000.

In October, McClellan was blamed for a humiliating setback at Ball's Bluff, Virginia, which demoralized the North badly. A reconnaissance in force turned into a rout in which Lincoln's close friend Edward D. Baker was killed. The news profoundly depressed the president, who was also dismayed by developments in the West. The commander in Missouri, John C. Frémont, was proving no better than McClellan. His tactlessness, poor judgment, egotism, ethical insensitivity, and general incompetence rendered him unfit for the job. During his first two months in Missouri, Frémont lost control of almost half the state as Confederates captured Lexington and whipped Union forces at the battle of Wilson's Creek.

Frémont's political mistakes proved more vexing to Lincoln than his military blunders. On August 30, without consulting the administration, he proclaimed martial law throughout Missouri and freed the slaves of disloyal masters. Though many Northerners applauded it, the emancipation order infuriated Kentuckians. When Lincoln gently urged Frémont to recall the emancipation order, the headstrong general balked, insisting that he would do so only in response to a direct presidential order. When Lincoln complied, his action touched off a fierce outburst of criticism. The poet James Russell Lowell spoke for many when he wondered, "How many times we are to save Kentucky and lose our self-respect?"[12] Ohio Senator Benjamin F. Wade indignantly declared that the president's softness on slavery "could only have come of one, born of 'poor white trash' and educated in a slave State."[13]

Conservative newspapers dismissed Lincoln's critics as "nigger-worshippers who have endeavored to make the struggle that has commenced a crusade against Southern institutions, in which oceans of blood should be shed to gratify the malice and folly of the school of which [William Lloyd] Garrison, [Horace] Greeley, Gerrit Smith, Wendell Phillips and others are the prominent representatives." Lincoln had "in his mild rebuke of Fremont" dealt "very tenderly" with the general. Those who "continue to glorify the imprudent proclamation of Fremont are counseling insubordination in its most dangerous form."[14]

When Lincoln received a protest from his conservative friend Orville H. Browning, he patiently explained that Frémont's "proclamation, as to confiscation of property, and the liberation of slaves, is *purely political*, and not within the range of military law, or necessity. If a commanding General finds a necessity to seize the farm of a private owner, for a pasture, an encampment, or a fortification, he has the right to do so, and to so hold it, as long as the necessity lasts; and this is within military law, because within military necessity. But to say the farm shall no longer belong to the owner, or his heirs forever; and this as well when the farm is not needed for military purposes as when it is, is purely political, without the savor of military law about it. And the same is true of slaves. If the General needs them, he can seize them, and use them; but when the need is past, it is not for him to fix their permanent future condition. That must be settled according to laws made by law-makers, and not by military proclamations. The proclamation in the point in question, is simply 'dictatorship.' . . . I cannot assume this reckless position; nor allow others to assume it on my responsibility. You speak of it as being the only means of *saving* the government. On the contrary it is itself the surrender of the government. Can it be pretended that it is any longer the government of the U.S.—any government of Constitution and laws,—wherein a General, or a President, may make permanent rules of property by proclamation?"[15]

Frémont's proclamation was as bad in practice as it was in theory: "No doubt the thing was popular in some quarters," Lincoln told Browning, "and would have been more so if it had been a general declaration of emancipation. The Kentucky Legislature would not budge till that proclamation was modified. . . . I was so assured, as to think it probable, that the very arms we had furnished Kentucky would be turned against us."[16] Lincoln was right in thinking that the public—especially in the Border States—was not yet ready to accept emancipation.

Lincoln received many complaints about Frémont's administrative ineptitude: the general was, they alleged, careless in letting out contracts, reclusive, obsessed with trivia, and incapable of making military plans. Even Frémont's admirers deplored his conduct.

Yet, Lincoln hesitated to dismiss Frémont because it was feared that "the army of the West would rebel."[17] But eventually even Lincoln's legendary patience wore thin. On October 24, after much dithering, he finally dismissed the general. In 1863, Lincoln told Hay, "I had thought well of Frémont. Even now I think well of his impulses. I only think he is the prey of wicked and designing men and I think he has absolutely no military capacity."[18]

Once again, Lincoln's treatment of Frémont aroused public anger. The editor of the *Cincinnati Gazette* warned that "the West is threatened with a revolution" because the "public consider that Fremont has been made a martyr." The general "is to the West what Napoleon was to France," and by firing him, Lincoln "has lost the confidence of the people."[19]

But the spirits of the Northern people were buoyed by the success of the Union navy, which in August gained control of Hatteras Inlet on North Carolina's Outer Banks and three months later captured Port Royal, South Carolina. The latter became an important base for the fleet enforcing the blockade.

Despite the good news from the Carolinas, Congress was in a foul mood when it reconvened in December. Impatient with McClellan, it established a Joint Committee on the Conduct of the War, which Radicals dominated. They adored the inept Frémont for his emancipation order and often chided Lincoln, who did not much mind, for the committee helped him goad timid generals into taking the offensive. The most conspicuous example of such a general was McClellan.

In early December, Lincoln quite reasonably suggested that McClellan attack the enemy's supply lines to Manassas. The general spurned that advice, protesting that Confederate forces greatly outnumbered his. Teasingly he stated that he did have a plan for an advance, but he would not disclose it. On December 20, he contracted typhoid fever, which sidelined him for three weeks. Meantime, the army entered winter quarters, much to the dismay of the North. People in Wisconsin, according to a Republican editor there, believed "that the President and Cabinet,—*as a whole,—are not equal to the occasion*."[20] On New Year's Eve, when the Committee on the Conduct of the War called at the White House, its chairman, Senator Wade, said, "Mr. President, you are murdering your country by inches in consequence of the inactivity of the military and the want of a distinct policy in regard to slavery."[21] Another Radical senator complained that Lincoln was "*timid* vacillating & inefficient."[22] The committee demanded a vigorous prosecution of the war in both the eastern and western theaters.

In the West, union commanders were no more aggressive than McClellan. In mid-November, after removing Frémont, Lincoln placed Henry W. Halleck, the country's leading military theorist, in command of the Department of Missouri, David Hunter in charge of the Department of Kansas, and Don Carlos Buell in command of the Department of the Ohio. Each proved a disappointment.

Halleck and Buell each offered abundant excuses for delay. Frustrated by Buell's failure to move toward East Tennessee to relieve the persecuted Unionists there, Lincoln asked the general to state when he could launch an offensive: "Delay is ruining us; and it is indispensable for me to have something definite."[23] He made a similar appeal to Halleck. When Halleck and Buell replied negatively, Lincoln told his secretary of war, "It is exceedingly discouraging. As everywhere else, nothing can be done."[24] In despair, the president asked Quartermaster General Montgomery Meigs, "[W]hat shall I do? The people are impatient; Chase has no money, and he tells me he can raise no more; the general of the army [McClellan] has typhoid fever. The bottom is out of the tub. What shall I do?"[25]

Much as McClellan's inaction exasperated Lincoln, equally troublesome was the action of a Union naval officer, Charles Wilkes, who touched off an international crisis by seizing two Confederate diplomats—John Slidell of Louisiana and James M. Mason of Virginia—as they sailed on the *Trent*, a British packet boat as it made its way from Cuba to Nassau. Wilkes stopped that vessel on the high seas and took the two emissaries prisoner, arguing that they were contraband of war, in effect animate messages sent from the Confederacy to Europe. Wilkes ignored maritime law, which required that the ship be taken to a port and the seizure of its property (including passengers) be adjudicated before a prize court. The Northern public rejoiced, especially since Mason and Slidell were notorious proslavery fire-eaters. At first, Lincoln shared his constituents' joy but quickly realized that the Union could scarcely afford to anger Great Britain and that the would-be emissaries had to be released.

In fact, Wilkes's action outraged the British government and public. The prime minister, Lord Palmerston, had a stern protest prepared, demanding not only that the envoys be released but also that the United States apologize and pay reparations. Queen Victoria and her husband, Prince Albert, toned down the document, but it remained bellicose. The Lincoln administration reluctantly concluded to release the prisoners in order to avoid war with Britain, though neither apology nor reparations were offered. Lincoln pithily summed up his thinking about the matter: "One war at a time." In persuading his advisors to go along with the unpopular decision, Lincoln had significant help from Charles Sumner, chairman of the Senate Foreign Relations Committee. The British were willing to forego reparations and apologies.

Lincoln described the surrender of Mason and Slidell as "a pretty bitter pill to swallow" but told an army officer that "I contented myself with believing that England's triumph in the matter would be short-lived, and that after ending our war successfully, we would be so powerful that we could call her to account for all the embarrassments she had inflicted upon us." The surrender made Lincoln feel "a great deal like the sick man in Illinois who was told he probably hadn't many days longer to live, and that he ought to make peace with any enemies he might have. He said the man he hated worst of all was a fellow named Brown in the next village and he guessed he had better begin on him. So Brown was sent for, and when he came the sick man began to say, in a voice 'as meek as Moses,' that he wanted to die at peace with all his fellow creatures, and he hoped he and Brown could now shake hands and bury all their enmity. The scene was becoming altogether too pathetic for Brown, who had to get out his handkerchief and wipe the gathering tears from his eyes. It wasn't long before he melted and gave his hand to his neighbor, and they had a regular love-feast. After a parting that would have softened the heart of a grindstone, Brown had about reached the room door, when the sick man rose up on his elbow and said, 'But, see here, Brown, if I *should* happen to get well, mind *that old grudge stands.*'"[26]

Months later, Lincoln told a visitor "how he had pushed the prompt surrender of Mason and Slidell as an act of justice to England, realizing that in light of international law the *Trent* affair might justly have given ground for reprisal. Seward would have temporized, and so risked a most unwelcome complication with England."[27] Just as he had done in May, Lincoln restrained his hotheaded secretary of state and helped avert a diplomatic rupture with Great Britain.

After the *Trent* crisis passed, Senator Sumner told Lincoln that if he had boldly addressed the slavery question, the administration would have enjoyed more support in Europe. In fact, Lincoln had been working behind the scenes to undermine slavery. In cooperation with antislavery leaders in Delaware, he drafted legislation providing federal subsidies to slaveholders in the First State if the legislature would abolish the peculiar institution. Lincoln hoped that if Delaware would do so, the other three loyal slave states—Maryland, Kentucky, and Missouri—would follow suit. He had high hopes, for the slave population in Delaware was quite small, and the legislature had come close to adopting gradual emancipation in 1847. But in early 1862, those hopes were dashed when the lawmakers in Delaware rejected the proposition.

When Congress reassembled in December 1861, Lincoln submitted his annual message (later such documents would be called state of the union addresses) that dealt cautiously with emancipation. Noting that the thousands of slaves in South Carolina and elsewhere who had come into Union lines existed in a kind of legal limbo, he suggested that they be colonized abroad. The same provision should be made for any Border States that emancipated their slaves, he recommended, and such states should be compensated by the federal government.

Abolitionists roundly condemned the colonization proposal, alleging that Lincoln suffered from "colorphobia." But he did not. He championed colonization because he realized that many whites would not accept emancipation unless it was accompanied by colonization. Eager to end slavery, he sought to sugarcoat the bitter pill of emancipation with colonization, compensation, and gradualism.

WAR IN EARNEST

A bolitionists also erupted in anger when Lincoln removed his incompetent secretary of war, Simon Cameron, after Cameron had recommended in his annual report that slaves be liberated and armed. Dismayed by this ill-timed proposal, Lincoln ordered Cameron to strike it from his report. The war secretary did so reluctantly but only after some newspapers published the original document. In January 1862, Lincoln dismissed Cameron, mainly because the Pennsylvania politico was simply not up to the job. To replace him, Lincoln chose another Pennsylvanian, Edwin M. Stanton, an eminent attorney who had served in the cabinet during the final weeks of James Buchanan's administration. The president demonstrated superhuman magnanimity in choosing Stanton, who had humiliated Lincoln in 1855 when they both served as counsel in a patent case. Then Stanton had viewed Lincoln as a contemptible provincial lawyer and snubbed him repeatedly.

Some Republicans objected to the nomination of a former Democrat like Stanton, but Lincoln said, "If I could find four more democrats just like Stanton, I would appoint them."[1] He remarked that "he knew him to be a true and loyal man, and that he possessed the greatest energy of character and systematic method in the discharge of public business."[2] Stanton proved an exceptionally able secretary of war and a devoted friend to Lincoln. A New York attorney told Lincoln of "the reviving confidence which your appointment of Mr Stanton had given us. The whole nation thanks God, that you had the wisdom and the courage to make the change."[3]

Stanton's appointment represented a key turning point in the war. The gruff new secretary of war infused energy into his department and the army. With his assistance, Lincoln began to assert himself more forcefully, showing less deference to timid generals. He studied military science as best he could and concluded sensibly that the North's superior manpower and economic strength were likely to prevail only if the enemy was pressed simultaneously on all fronts. In January 1862, he wrote to Don Carlos Buell, "I state my general idea of this war to be that we have the *greater* numbers, and the enemy has the *greater* facility of concentrating forces upon points of collision; that we must fail, unless we can find some way of making *our* advantage an over-match for *his*; and that this can only be done by menacing him with superior forces at *different* points, at the *same* time; so that we can safely attack, one, or both, if he makes no change; and if he *weakens* one to *strengthen* the other, forbear to attack the strengthened one, but seize, and hold the weakened one, gaining so much."[4]

Lincoln was not obsessed by a desire to wield power, but he took seriously his oath of office and conscientiously performed what he considered to be his duty, no matter how onerous that might be. He called the presidency "a big job," about which "the country little knows how big." To an Illinois friend, he confided, "This getting the nomination for President, and being elected, is all very pleasant to a man's ambition; but to be the President, and to meet the responsibilities and discharge the duties of the office in times like these is anything but pleasant. I would gladly if I could, take my neck from the yoke, and go home with you to Springfield, and live, as I used, in peace with my friends, than to endure this harassing kind of life."[5]

Soon after Stanton took office and Lincoln began to assert himself, the North started to win significant victories everywhere but the East. In January, Union troops defeated the Confederates at Mill Springs, Kentucky. The following month, General Ambrose E. Burnside captured Roanoke Island in North Carolina and, far more important, Ulysses S. Grant and Admiral Andrew Hull Foote took Forts Henry and Donelson in Tennessee, opening the way for an invasion of the southwestern Confederacy. Upon hearing the news about Donelson, where several thousand Confederates were taken prisoner, a Washingtonian exulted, "Our hearts are bursting with gratitude, our tears start, we grasp hands, we laugh, we say 'God be thanked;' our country's honor is vindicated, the stain of our Flag is forever blotted out!"[6]

Lincoln had labored hard to make sure that Grant and Foote had floating mortars, saying, "I am going to devote a part of every day to these mortars and I won[']t leave off until it fairly rains Bombs."[7] The tough-minded president remarked that he desired "to rain the Rebels out" and "treat them to a refreshing shower of sulphur and brimstone."[8] Lincoln was famously charitable, mild-mannered, and merciful, but he was also a passionately committed war leader who infused his steely determination into the North.

Always intrigued by things mechanical, Lincoln took a special interest in weaponry and encouraged the development of small arms, artillery, flamethrowers, rockets, submarines, mines, ironclad ships, and explosives. He even tested rifles personally and urged the adoption of breechloaders, repeaters, and an early version of the machine gun. When the stuffy War Department bureaucracy balked, he did his best to get it to change its hidebound ways; he was only partially successful.

Lincoln also tried to goad George B. McClellan into action, also with partial success. In early January, acting on Montgomery Meigs's advice, he summoned the division commanders of the Army of the Potomac for a conference, saying that if McClellan did not want to use the army, he would like to borrow it. Upon learning of this conference, McClellan, who had been laid up with typhoid, suddenly felt better and insisted that he intended to go on the offensive but refused to share his plan with Lincoln, who responded by issuing a highly unusual set of War Orders. The first, dated January 27, stipulated that all land and naval forces must move against the Confederates on February 22. John Hay noted that this document, known as "President's General War Order No. 1," represented a significant departure: "He wrote it without any consultation and read it to the Cabinet, not for their sanction but for their information. From that time he influenced actively the operations of the Campaign. He stopped going to McClellan's and sent for the general to come to him. Every thing grew busy and animated after this order."[9] Other war orders followed, prompting McClellan finally to disclose his plan, which was to attack Richmond from the east. That required shipping the army down the Chesapeake Bay to a site on the Rappahannock River.

Lincoln demurred, arguing that it would be better to attack the lines supplying the enemy at Manassas. Since the Confederates had to be attacked somewhere, it made more sense to do so at Manassas, where their supply lines were longer and the Union's supply lines shorter. But McClellan was adamant, and Lincoln reluctantly acquiesced with the understanding that a sufficiently large force would be left to defend Washington in case the enemy should attack it while McClellan was sailing toward Richmond. Though the general agreed to do so, he in fact deployed only a token force to protect Washington. Later, when Lincoln discovered how inadequate that force was, he insisted that the part of McClellan's army corps commanded by Irvin McDowell march overland toward the Confederate capital, thus acting as a shield protecting Washington. Furious at this change of plans to have McDowell sail with the rest of the army to the peninsula, McClellan protested heatedly but in vain.

In March, the Army of the Potomac launched what became known as the Peninsula Campaign, for McClellan had altered his strategy when the Confederates abandoned Manassas and withdrew southward. Instead of landing on the Rappahannock River at Urbanna, he would transport his army to Fort Monroe, at the tip of the Virginia peninsula formed by the York and James Rivers. He would move up the peninsula, then swing west toward Richmond. When he encountered resistance at Yorktown in March and April, McClellan grossly overestimated the size of John A. Magruder's Confederate force, which he could easily have swept aside if he had attacked. Instead, he wasted a month preparing to mount a siege. In that time, General Joseph E. Johnston shifted his Rebel forces to the peninsula. Upon observing Magruder's small command, Johnston declared, "No one but McClellan could have hesitated to attack."[10] Lincoln said, "[T]here was no reason why he [McClellan] should have been detained a single day at Yorktown, but he waited and gave the enemy time to gather his forces and strengthen his position."[11]

When McClellan finally drew near the Confederate capital, he fought an indecisive battle at Fair Oaks in early June. There Johnston was so badly wounded that he had to be replaced. Fatefully, Confederate President Jefferson Davis chose Robert E. Lee as Johnston's successor. McClellan rejoiced, for he described the new enemy commander as "too cautious & weak under grave responsibility" and "wanting in moral firmness when pressed by heavy responsibility & is likely to be timid & irresolute in action."[12] As the subsequent fighting revealed, those flaws were McClellan's, not Lee's.

Realizing that he would lose if he simply waited for McClellan to attack with his superior numbers, Lee decided to take the offensive. Boldly he sent Stonewall Jackson's corps up the Shenandoah Valley toward Washington. If McClellan had attacked while Jackson was thus occupied, he might have easily defeated the remainder of Lee's army. But Little Mac did not do so. As Jackson proceeded northward, Lincoln took a gamble. Believing that if McDowell could swing west to cut off Jackson's line of retreat, the Confederates could be defeated handily. So instead of having McDowell march southward to link up with McClellan, Lincoln ordered some units of that corps to proceed into the valley and "bag" Jackson, in cooperation with other Union forces in the area. This tactic may have worked if the division commanders had moved swiftly, but they did not, and Jackson escaped to rejoin the Army of Northern Virginia by late June. Then, in a series of battles collectively known as the Seven Days, Lee drove the Army of the Potomac away from the gates of Richmond all the way to Harrison's Landing on the James.

It was a humiliating defeat, which McClellan blamed on Lincoln. As Little Mac retreated to his defensive position, he sent Stanton a telegram full of his usual appeals for reinforcements and closing with a remarkable accusation: "If I save this army now, I tell you plainly that I owe no thanks to you or to any other persons in Washington. You have done your best to sacrifice this army."[13] (A scandalized telegrapher took it upon himself to omit those inflammatory words.)

This was a grossly unfair charge, for Lincoln and Stanton had done all they could to supply McClellan with men and materiel. Even if McDowell's corps had not been diverted, it is highly unlikely that the timid McClellan could have defeated Lee. Indeed, he had a glorious chance to capture Richmond after Malvern Hill, the final battle of the Seven Days, but he failed to take advantage of his opportunity. Weeks later, Lincoln remarked that McClellan "is well versed in military matters, and has had opportunities of experience and observation. Still there must be something wrong somewhere, and I'll tell you what it is, *he never embraces his opportunities*,—that's where the trouble is—he always puts off the hour for embracing his opportunities."[14]

After the defeat of McClellan's peninsula campaign, the public clamored for a more vigorous prosecution of the war. A Kansan spoke for many when he declared, "Lincoln has pursued the policy of conciliation long enough. He has given it a fair trial."[15] The president agreed: "I have got done throwing grass." From now on, he "proposed trying stones."[16] Pointedly he asked supporters of a conciliatory policy: should the war be fought "with elder-stalk squirts, charged with rose water?"[17]

To implement his new "hard war" policy, Lincoln placed John Pope in charge of the forces in the Shenandoah Valley and ordered McClellan to transfer his army from Harrison's Landing to Pope's base on the Rappahannock. While Little Mac slowly carried out this order, Lee boldly attacked Pope and won a smashing victory at the Second Battle of Bull Run in late August. Lincoln was furious at McClellan for deliberately dawdling in an attempt to make sure that Pope would be defeated. By the time Lee attacked, only twenty-five thousand men of the Army of the Potomac's ninety thousand had reached Pope's base. As the battle raged, McClellan sent the president an astounding telegram: "I am clear that one of two courses should be adopted. 1st To concentrate all our available forces to open communication with Pope—2nd To leave Pope to get out of his scrape & at once use all our means to make the Capital perfectly safe."[18] This message convinced Lincoln "that McC[lellan] wanted Pope defeated." The president "seemed to think him [McClellan] a little crazy."[19] (McClellan in fact suffered from paranoia, which led him to see enemies everywhere and made him quarrelsome, mistrustful, secretive, harshly judgmental, rigid, and self-righteous. In addition, he was an envious, arrogant, and grandiose narcissist.)[20]

Lincoln told Secretary of the Navy Gideon Welles that "there has been a design, a purpose in breaking down Pope, without regard of consequences to the country. It is shocking to see and know this." On August 30, he added, "We had the enemy in the hollow of our hands" and would have destroyed him "if our generals, who are vexed with Pope, had done their duty. All of our present difficulties and reverses have been brought upon us by these quarrels of the generals."[21] Lincoln did not give way to despair. On September 1, Hay noted in his diary that the president "was in a singularly defiant tone of mind. He often repeated, 'We must hurt this enemy before it gets away.'" When Hay observed that the situation looked grim, Lincoln replied, "No, Mr Hay, we must whip these people now. Pope must fight them, if they are too strong for him he can gradually retire to these fortifications." Hay believed it was thanks to Lincoln's "indomitable will, that army movements have been characterized by such energy and celerity for the last few days."[22]

Pope did fall back to Washington, where Lincoln found the army badly demoralized. To restore morale, the president reluctantly appointed McClellan to take charge of the city's defenses. When cabinet members objected, Lincoln replied that McClellan "knows this whole ground—his specialty is to defend—he is a good engineer, all admit—there is no better organizer—he can be trusted to act on the defensive, but having the 'slows' he is good for nothing for an onward movement."[23]

After Lee crossed the Potomac into Maryland, Lincoln asked Little Mac to resume command of the Army of the Potomac. In that capacity, the general demonstrated that he did indeed have a case of the "slows." His glacial pursuit of the Army of Northern Virginia culminated in the Battle of Antietam on September 17. McClellan could have won a smashing victory if he had marched faster or if he had thrown in all his men during the battle. As it was, the two armies in effect fought a standoff. But because Lee withdrew from the field and recrossed the Potomac, the outcome was widely regarded as a Union triumph.

DEALING WITH SLAVERY

A ntietam represented a crucial turning point in the war, for that quasi-victory enabled Lincoln to announce publicly his intention to issue an Emancipation Proclamation. Shortly after the Peninsula Campaign ended, he had read to the cabinet a document stating that "as a fit and necessary military measure for effecting this object [i.e., restoration of the Union] I, as Commander-in-Chief of the Army and Navy of the United States, do order and declare that on the first day of January in the year of Our Lord one thousand, eight hundred and sixty three, all persons held as slaves within any state or states, wherein the constitutional authority of the United States shall not then be practically recognized, shall then, thenceforward and forever, be free."[1]

Months earlier, Lincoln had asked Congress to appropriate money to compensate slaveholders in any of the loyal Border States (Maryland, Delaware, Missouri, and Kentucky) that agreed to abolish slavery. Over the next several weeks, he repeatedly urged congressmen and senators from those states to support his plan of gradual, compensated emancipation, but they refused, as did their state legislatures. In July 1862, Congress passed the Second Confiscation Act, freeing the slaves of disloyal owners. That impractical statute would have required court proceedings to determine the loyalty of slave owners. Lincoln feared that the law violated the Constitutional ban on bills of attainder and ex post facto laws, so Congress amended the bill to meet his objections.

Secretary of State William Henry Seward warned that promulgating an emancipation measure just after the defeat of the Peninsula Campaign would seem like an insincere, desperation gesture. Impressed by that argument, Lincoln shelved the document and awaited a Union victory. Five days after the Battle of Antietam, when he was sure that it could in fact be considered a victory, Lincoln publicly declared his intention to issue a proclamation on January 1 that would free slaves in areas that were still in rebellion but not in the loyal Border States or in portions of the Confederacy already in Union hands. Lincoln limited the scope of emancipation because the proclamation could be justified constitutionally only on grounds of military necessity: to free the slaves of rebellious owners would undermine the ability of the Confederacy to wage war. Lincoln stated that "he had power to issue the proclamation only in virtue of his power to strike at the rebellion, and he could not include places within our own lines, because the reason upon which the power depended did not apply to them, and he could not include such places" just because he opposed slavery himself.[2]

The cold, legalistic language of the proclamation disappointed many Radicals, including Frederick Douglass, who complained that it "touched neither justice nor mercy. Had there been one expression of sound moral feeling against Slavery, one word of regret and shame that this accursed system had remained so long the disgrace and scandal of the Republic, one word of satisfaction in the hope of burying slavery and the rebellion in one common grave, a thrill of joy would have run around the world."[3]

Lincoln had employed dry verbiage in the Emancipation Proclamation deliberately, for he did not want to antagonize conservatives, and he wished to give slaves freed by the proclamation a solid legal basis for their freedom in case the proclamation was challenged in court. Lincoln said that he was "strongly pressed" to justify the document "upon high moral grounds, and to introduce into the instrument unequivocal language testifying to the negroes' right to freedom upon the precise principles expounded by the Emancipationists of both Old and New-England." He rejected such counsel, for "policy requires that the Proclamation be issued as a war measure, and not a measure of morality; and that Law and Justice require that the slaves should be enabled to plead the Proclamation hereafter if necessary to establish judicially their title to freedom. They can do this, the President says, on a proclamation proceeding as a war measure from the Commander-in-Chief of the Army, but not on one issuing from the bosom of philanthropy."[4]

In his annual message to Congress in December 1862, Lincoln employed the eloquent rhetoric that critics missed in the Emancipation Proclamation: "The dogmas of the quiet past, are inadequate to the stormy present. The occasion is piled high with difficulty, and we must rise to the occasion. As our case is new, so we must think and act anew. We must disenthrall ourselves, and then we shall save our country. Fellow citizens, we cannot escape history. We of this Congress and this administration, will be remembered in spite of ourselves. No personal significance, or insignificance, can spare one or another of us. The fiery trial through which we pass, will light us down, in honor or dishonor, to the latest generation. We say we are for the Union. The world will not forget that we say this. We know how to save the Union. The world knows we do know how to save it. We—even *we here*—hold the power, and bear the responsibility. In *giving* freedom to the *slave*, we *assure* freedom to the *free*—honorable alike in what we give, and what we preserve. We shall nobly save, or meanly lose, the last best hope of earth."[5]

Three weeks after the proclamation was issued, Lincoln said that it had "knocked the bottom out of slavery," but he did not expect "any sudden results from it."[6] Though not sudden, the results would be profound. He considered the promulgation of the document "the central act of my administration" as well as "the great event of the nineteenth century" and predicted accurately that "that the name which is connected with this matter will never be forgotten."[7]

Massachusetts Governor John A. Andrew called the Emancipation Proclamation "a mighty *act*" though a "poor *document*," "slow, somewhat halting, wrong in its delay till January, but great and sublime after all."[8] "We shout for joy that we live to record this righteous decree," wrote Douglass. Though Lincoln might be slow, Douglass was positive that the president was "not the man to reconsider, retract and contradict words and purposes solemnly proclaimed over his official signature."[9] *Harper's Weekly* declared that there "was a time, not very long since, when a large majority of the Northern people would have opposed it [the Emancipation Proclamation] strenuously, not so much from admiration of slavery, as from the belief that, under the Constitution, we had no right to meddle with it, and that its abolition involved dangers and inconveniences perhaps as formidable as those that were created by its existence. Even at the present time a mortal antipathy for the negro is entertained by a large class of persons at the North. . . . Demagogues will of course endeavor to excite our working-classes against the Government by threatening them with the competition of free negro labor."[10]

In fact, Democrats used that demagogic argument effectively during the fall election campaigns. The Emancipation Proclamation hurt the Republican party, which suffered heavy losses. When Lincoln had informed the cabinet about his plan to issue an Emancipation Proclamation, Postmaster General Montgomery Blair, a committed emancipationist, presciently argued that there was "no public sentiment at the North, even among extreme men which now demands the proposed measure." The proclamation, he said, would "endanger our power in Congress, and put the power in the next House of Representatives in the hands of those opposed to the war, or to our mode of carrying it on."[11] Democrats called the proclamation "a nullity," a "monstrous usurpation," a "criminal wrong," and an "act of national suicide" that would "excite the ridicule that follows impotency."[12] The *New York Evening Express* insisted that no human mind ever "conceived a policy so well fitted, utterly to degrade and destroy white labor, and to reduce the white man to the level of the negro."[13]

Democrats played the race card endlessly, causing Republicans to denounce "that cruel and ungenerous prejudice against color which still remains to disgrace our civilization and to impeach our Christianity."[14] With justice, the *Cincinnati Commercial* lamented that "the prejudice of race has been inflamed, and used by the Democratic party with an energy and ingenuity perfectly infernal."[15] Democratic newspapers warned Ohio workingmen that they might "have to leave Ohio and labor where niggers could not come" and called upon them to support Democratic candidates if they did "not desire their place occupied by negroes."[16] To Salmon P. Chase, a Republican congressional candidate in Ohio described his defeat: "I had thought until this year the cry of 'nigger' & 'abolitionism' were played out, but they never had as much power & effect in this part of the State as at the recent election. Many who had heretofore acted with us voted the straight democratic ticket."[17] Former Ohio Governor William Allen declared, "Every white laboring man in the North who does not want to be swapped off for a free nigger should vote the Democratic ticket." If the slaves were emancipated, he warned, thousands of them, "with their hands reeking in the blood of murdered women and children," would "cross over into our state" seeking employment.[18]

CHAPTER EIGHT

WINTER OF DISCONTENT

In addition to the racist backlash against emancipation, a lack of military success helped defeat Republicans at the polls in November. After Antietam, Lincoln urged McClellan to pursue Lee vigorously, but Little Mac offered myriad excuses for not moving. Six weeks after the battle, when McClellan complained that he could not advance because his horses were fatigued, Lincoln wired him, "I have just received your dispatch about sore tongued and fatiegued horses. Will you pardon me for asking what the horses of your army have done since the battle of Antietam that fatigue anything?"[1] Disgusted, Lincoln called the Army of the Potomac "McClellan's bodyguard."[2]

On October 13, Lincoln bluntly wrote McClellan, "You remember my speaking to you of what I called your over-cautiousness. Are you not over-cautious when you assume that you can not do what the enemy is constantly doing? Should you not claim to be at least his equal in prowess, and act upon the claim?"[3]

Even though he had tried to warn the general that he must advance or else lose his job, Lincoln expressed doubt that McClellan "would move after all" and added that "he'd got tired of his excuses" and "*he'd remove him at once but for the election.*"[4]

Immediately after the November elections, Lincoln finally did remove McClellan, explaining that he "had tried long enough to bore with an auger too dull to take hold." He added, "I said I would remove him if he let Lee's army get away from him, and I must do so.

He has got the 'slows.'"[5] McClellan's most thoughtful biographer called him "inarguably the worst" of the generals who commanded the Army of the Potomac.[6]

Lincoln's unsuccessful efforts to goad McClellan into action reminded the president of a story: "I was not more successful than the blacksmith in our town, in my boyhood days, when he tried to put to a useful purpose a big piece of wrought-iron that was in the shop. He heated it up, put it on the anvil, and said: 'I'm going to make a sledge-hammer out of you.' After a while he stopped hammering it, looked at it, and remarked: 'Guess I've drawed you out a little too fine for a sledge-hammer; reckon I'd better make a clevis of you.' He stuck it in the fire, blew the bellows, got up a good heat, then began shaping the iron again on the anvil. Pretty soon he stopped, sized it up with his eye, and said: 'Guess I've drawed you out too thin for a clevis; suppose I better make a clevis-bolt of you.' He put it in the fire. Bore down still harder on the bellows, drew out the iron, and went to work at it once more on the anvil. In a few minutes he stopped, took a look, and exclaimed: 'Well, now I've got you a leetle too thin even to make a clevis-bolt out of you.' Then he rammed it in the fire again, threw his whole weight on top of the bellows, got up a white heat on the iron, jerked it out, carried it in the tongs to the water-barrel, held it over the barrel, and cried: 'I've tried to make a sledge-hammer of you, and failed; I've tried to make a clevis of you, and failed; I've tried to make a clevis-bolt of you, and failed; now, darn you, I'm going to make a fizzle of you'; and with that he soused it in the water and let it fizz."[7]

To replace Little Mac, Lincoln chose the senior corps commander in the Army of the Potomac, Ambrose E. Burnside, who had earlier turned down the position, protesting that he was not competent to lead the army. (Later events would prove that he was right.)

Writing from Illinois two weeks before the November elections, a friend told Lincoln, "If we are beaten in this State, it will be because McClellan and Buell *won't fight*."[8] Don Carlos Buell was in effect the McClellan of the western theater. In the summer of 1862, when Confederate General Braxton Bragg led his men into Kentucky, Buell abandoned plans to relieve eastern Tennessee in order to protect Louisville and Cincinnati. But he seemed to avoid confronting Bragg, who captured a total of eight thousand Union troops at two garrisons. Lincoln goaded Buell into pursuing Bragg more seriously, and finally, on October 8, the two armies clashed at Perryville, Kentucky. Bragg fell back to Tennessee, but Buell failed to pursue him vigorously. Salmon P. Chase joked that the planet Earth was "a body of considerable magnitude—but moves faster than Gen. Buell."[9]

Lincoln sent instructions to Buell through the War Department, which notified the general that the president "does not understand why we cannot march as the enemy marches, live as he lives, and fight as he fights, unless we admit the inferiority of our troops and of our generals."[10] On October 24, Lincoln finally dismissed Buell, replacing him with William S. Rosecrans. Henry W. Halleck, who had recently been appointed commander of all Union armies, told Rosecrans (reflecting Lincoln's view) that the "time has now come when we must apply the sterner rules of war, whenever such application becomes necessary, to enable us to support our armies and to move them rapidly upon the enemy. You will not hesitate to do this in all cases where the exigencies of the war require it. . . . Neither the country nor the Government will much longer put up with the inactivity of some of our armies and generals."[11]

In early December 1862, Congress reconvened in a sour mood. "It seems to me that this is the darkest day yet, and no ray of light as yet penetrates the thick clouds which hang over us," Representative Henry L. Dawes of Massachusetts wrote from Washington on December 10. "There is no change for the better here. We have reached this state of things for want of capacity and that can't be supplied."[12]

Three days later, the gloom thickened when Burnside, for want of capacity, led the Army of the Potomac to ignominious defeat at the Battle of Fredericksburg. The Union suffered twelve thousand casualties, the Confederates less than half as many. In despair, Lincoln moaned, "if there is a worse place than hell I am in it."[13]

Making life even more hellish for Lincoln, Senate Republicans demanded that Seward be removed from the cabinet. Chase had been filling the senators' ears with tales of Seward's malign influence on the president. According to the treasury secretary, the cabinet met seldom, and Seward dominated Lincoln, urging him to adopt the conservative policies and appointments that had led to Union defeats. Hearing of this attempted putsch, Seward promptly offered his resignation, lest his continued service as secretary of state embarrass the administration. The president was extremely reluctant to accept the resignation, for Seward represented the large conservative faction of the Republican party. If he were gone, the leading Radical in that body, Chase, would dominate it. Moreover, Lincoln liked Seward, who had proved an able secretary of state. What to do?

Lincoln finessed this threat to Republican unity skillfully by inviting the senators to the White House for a conference. After listening to their complaints, he said he would consider what they had to say and invited them back for another meeting the following day. To their surprise, the senators found at the second meeting the entire cabinet (minus Seward) in attendance. When Lincoln invited the lawmakers to repeat their charges, most cabinet members denied them, placing Chase in an awkward position. Either he had to contradict his colleagues or acknowledge that he had misled the senators. As he fumbled awkwardly to find some middle ground between those two positions, the senators felt deceived and embarrassed.

The next day, Chase called on Lincoln and "said he had been painfully affected by the meeting last evening, which was a total surprise to him, and, after some not very explicit remarks as to how he was affected, informed the President he had prepared his resignation."

Eagerly Lincoln asked, "Where is it?"

"I brought it with me," said Chase. "I wrote it this morning."

"Let me have it," demanded the president.

Lincoln tore open the envelope. "This cuts the Gordian knot," he said. "I can dispose of this subject now without difficulty. I see my way clear."[14] Shortly thereafter, he told a senator, "Now I can ride: I have a pumpkin in each end of my bag."[15]

Lincoln's brilliant tactical maneuver allowed him to weather one of the gravest political crises of the war. Later he told John Hay, "I do not now see how it could have been done better. I am sure it was right. If I had yielded to that storm & dismissed Seward the thing would all have slumped over one way & we should have been left with a scanty handful of supporters. When Chase sent in his resignation I saw that the game was in my own hands & I put it through."[16]

Discussing the senators' attempted putsch, Lincoln said, "It was very well to talk of remodeling the Cabinet, but the caucus had thought more of *their* plans than of *his* benefit, and he told them so."[17] Customarily, Lincoln sought to treat opponents fairly, and he wanted them to reciprocate. When confronted with a difficult case, he said, "I always try to understand both sides, and begin by putting myself into the shoes of the party against whom I feel a prejudice; but then I expect that party to get into mine, so that he may also feel my responsibility."[18]

In the aftermath of the cabinet crisis, one of its leading participants, Maine Senator William P. Fessenden, wrote that if "all men upon whom we have a right to rely [had] proved brave & true and forgotten themselves in their love of country, I think it [the putsch attempt] would have been productive of great good." He was especially disappointed at "the weak squeamishness of our friend Chase," who, he said, lacked "nerve and force." Fessenden speculated that the treasury secretary "will never be forgiven by many for deliberately sacrificing his friends to the fear of offending his & their enemies. To him it is owing that the Cabinet remains as it is—admitted by him to be weak, divided, vacillating and powerless." But, the senator acknowledged, Lincoln "thinks he cannot get along without Seward, and, really, it would be very difficult to supply his place at this juncture. For, though I have little confidence in him, still he represents a great and powerful army of friends." Moreover, the country's "foreign affairs are too complicated" to entrust to a new man.[19]

Bitterly distraught by the defeat at Fredericksburg, Lincoln took some comfort from the quasi-victory that Union General Rosecrans won over Bragg at the Battle of Stones River (December 31–January 2) in Tennessee. Like Antietam, Union and Confederate forces fought what was essentially a draw, but Bragg withdrew from the field, giving the advantage to the North. (Later, Ulysses S. Grant remarked that Stones River was something of a Pyrrhic victory: "A few such fights would have ruined us.")[20] Vastly relieved, Lincoln congratulated Rosecrans, "God bless you and all with you!" Months later, he told Old Rosy, "[Y]ou gave us a hard earned victory which, had there been a defeat instead, the nation could scarcely have lived over." The Battle of Stones River had checked "a dangerous sentiment which was spreading in the north."[21]

Lincoln also derived some consolation from the knowledge that even though Union losses at Fredericksburg were severe, they could be more readily replaced than the Confederate losses. He said that "if the same battle were to be fought over again, every day, through a week of days, with the same relative results, the army under Lee would be wiped out to its last man, the Army of the Potomac would still be a mighty host, the war would be over, the Confederacy gone, and peace would be won at a smaller cost of life than it will be if the week of lost battles must be dragged out through yet another year of camps and marches, and of deaths in hospitals, rather than upon the field. No general yet found can face the arithmetic; but the end of the war will be at hand when he shall be discovered."[22]

Lincoln hoped that Joseph Hooker might be that general, for in January 1863 the president chose him to replace Burnside. Lincoln had some reservations about "Fighting Joe," which he spelled out in a remarkable document, full of wise paternal advice, that he gave the general upon his promotion to command of the Army of the Potomac: "I have placed you at the head of the Army of the Potomac. Of course I have done this upon what appear to me to be sufficient reasons. And yet I think it best for you to know that there are some things in regard to which, I am not quite satisfied with you. I believe you to be a brave and a skilful soldier, which, of course, I like. I also believe you do not mix politics with your profession, in which you are right. You have confidence in yourself, which is a valuable, if not an indispensable quality. You are ambitious, which, within reasonable bounds, does good rather than harm. But I think that during Gen. Burnside's command of the Army, you have taken counsel of your ambition, and thwarted him as much as you could, in which you did a great wrong to the country, and to a most meritorious and honorable brother officer. I have heard, in such way as to believe it, of your recently saying that both the Army and the Government needed a Dictator. Of course it was not *for* this, but in spite of it, that I have given you the command. Only those generals who gain successes, can set up dictators. What I now ask of you is military success, and I will risk the dictatorship." In closing, Lincoln urged Hooker to "beware of rashness. *Beware of rashness*, but with energy, and sleepless vigilance, go forward, and give us victories."[23]

While Hooker whipped the demoralized army into shape and devised a brilliant offensive plan for it, other Union commanders fared badly. In April, Admiral Samuel F. Du Pont's naval assault on Charleston, South Carolina, failed, much to Lincoln's dismay if not surprise. Weeks before the assault, he had remarked that Du Pont "is everlastingly asking for more . . . ironclads. He will do nothing with any. He has intelligence and system, and will maintain a good blockade," but "he will never take Sumter or get to Charleston."[24] In the early months of 1863, Grant's campaign against Vicksburg, Mississippi, was stalled, as was N. P. Banks's effort to capture Port Hudson, Louisiana. Rosecrans had gone into winter quarters without following up his advantage after Stones River.

Coming on top of these disappointments, Hooker's defeat at the Battle of Chancellorsville, Virginia, in early May caused Lincoln to despair. When he received word of the terrible thrashing that the Army of the Potomac took at the hands of Lee, he tearfully exclaimed, "My God! my God! What will the country say? What will the country say?"[25] An Ohio senator reported that Lincoln "is subject to the deepest depression of spirits amounting to Monomania. He looked upon Hooker as his 'last card.'"[26] The president told a caller, "I am the loneliest man in America."[27]

THE TIDE TURNS

Offsetting bad news from the Virginia front was good news from the West. In May, Grant had boldly marched his troops south of Vicksburg, crossed the Mississippi River, and fought one successful battle after another. Lincoln exclaimed, "This is more important than anything which is occurring in Virginia! I have had stronger influence brought against Grant, praying for his removal, since the battle of Pittsburg Landing, than for any other object, coming too from good men."[1] (In April 1862, Grant was widely condemned for being unprepared for the Confederate assault at the Battle of Shiloh—also known as Pittsburg Landing, in Tennessee. Lincoln told a friend, "Do you know that at one time I stood solitary and alone here in favor of General Grant.")[2] But, Lincoln continued, "now look at his campaign since May 1. Where is anything like it in the Old World that equals it? It stamps him as the greatest general of the age, if not of the world."[3] On July 4, after a prolonged siege, Grant finally captured the citadel of Vicksburg, Mississippi, and the entire Confederate army defending it.

Modestly, Lincoln congratulated Grant "for the almost inestimable service" he had done the country: "When you first reached the vicinity of Vicksburg, I thought you should do, what you finally did—march the troops across the neck, run the batteries with the transports, and thus go below; and I never had any faith, except a general hope that you knew better than I, that the Yazoo Pass expedition, and the like, could succeed. When you got below, and took Port-Gibson, Grand

Gulf, and vicinity, I thought you should go down the river and join Gen. [N. P.] Banks; and when you turned Northward East of the Big Black, I feared it was a mistake. I now wish to make the personal acknowledgment that you were right, and I was wrong."[4]

Nine days after the fall of Vicksburg, Banks took Port Hudson, Louisiana. Helping him were black troops, who had joined the army earlier in 1863 after the administration reversed its earlier policy of forbidding black men to enlist. Thus the Mississippi River was completely in Union hands. Confederate states west of the river—Arkansas, Texas, and Louisiana—were cut off, and (as Lincoln put it), the "Father of Waters" was once again able to flow "unvexed to the sea."[5] The president gratefully told Banks that the "final stroke in opening the Mississippi never should, and I think never will, be forgotten."[6]

As those momentous victories were being won in the West, the Army of the Potomac finally triumphed over Robert E. Lee. Even though Lee had lost Stonewall Jackson, his ablest corps commander, at the Battle of Chancellorsville, the Confederate commander decided once again to invade the North. On June 27, as the Army of Northern Virginia was moving toward Pennsylvania, Joseph Hooker impetuously resigned when Henry W. Halleck and Edwin M. Stanton countermanded one of his orders. Upon receipt of Hooker's dispatch, Lincoln grew pale.

Stanton asked, "What shall be done?"

Lincoln said, "Accept his resignation."[7]

Salmon P. Chase objected, but the president cut him off: "The acceptance of an army resignation is not a matter for your department."[8] (Here Lincoln demonstrated what John Hay called the "tyrannous authority" that the president exercised over his cabinet.)[9]

In choosing Hooker's successor, Lincoln resisted appeals to reinstate McClellan and instead selected a senior corps commander, George Gordon Meade, a native of Pennsylvania. Lincoln quipped that Meade, like a gamecock, would "fight well on his own dunghill."[10] And so he did. At the small town of Gettysburg, Pennsylvania, during the first three days of July, Lee and Meade fought the bloodiest battle of the war. Lee lost one-third of his men (twenty-eight thousand) while Meade lost one-fifth of his (twenty-three thousand).

Grateful as he was for the victory at Gettysburg, Lincoln was dismayed by Meade's announcement that his men would "drive from our soil every vestige of the presence of the invader."

"Drive the invader from our soil! My God! Is that all?" Lincoln asked incredulously.[11] He called it "a dreadful reminiscence of McClellan. The same spirit that moved McC. to claim a great victory because P[ennsylvani]a and M[arylan]d were safe." Exasperated, he declared, "Will our Generals never get that idea out of their heads? The whole country is *our* soil."[12]

On July 4, as Grant was accepting the surrender of Vicksburg, Robert E. Lee began retreating from Gettysburg and headed toward Virginia. Lincoln urged Meade to pursue Lee and destroy the Army of Northern Virginia before it could cross the rain-swollen Potomac River. Over the next ten days, Meade, however, dawdled and allowed the Confederates to escape, much to Lincoln's chagrin.

During those anxious days, Lincoln spent a great deal of time at the War Department, where a telegrapher watched him closely. Lincoln's "anxiety seemed as great as it had been during the battle itself," the telegrapher recalled; he "walked up and down the floor, his face grave and anxious, wringing his hands and showing every sign of deep solicitude. As the telegrams came in, he traced the positions of the two armies on the map, and several times called me up to point out their location, seeming to feel the need of talking to some one. Finally, a telegram came from Meade saying that under such and such circumstances he would engage the enemy at such and such a time. 'Yes,' said the president bitterly, 'he will be ready to fight a magnificent battle when there is no enemy there to fight!'"[13]

On July 14, when it was learned that Lee had successfully crossed the Potomac unharmed, Lincoln moaned, "We only had to stretch forth our hands & they were ours. And nothing I could say or do could make the Army move."[14] Robert Todd Lincoln reported that his father, with tears in his eyes, "grieved silently but deeply about the escape of Lee. He said, 'If I had gone up there I could have whipped them myself.'"[15] The president agreed with his close friend David Davis, who called Lee's escape "one of the great disasters & humiliations of the war."[16]

Lincoln wrote Meade a harsh letter: "You fought and beat the enemy at Gettysburg; and, of course, to say the least, his loss was as great as yours. He retreated; and you did not, as it seemed to me, pressingly pursue him; but a flood in the river detained him, till, by slow degrees, you were again upon him. . . . you stood and let the flood run down, bridges be built, and the enemy move away at his leisure, without attacking him. . . . He was within your easy grasp, and to have closed upon him would, in connection with our other late successes, have ended the war. As it is, the war will be prolonged indefinitely. . . . Your golden opportunity is gone, and I am distressed immeasureably because of it."[17] Wisely, Lincoln did not send Meade this rebuke but instead filed it away, unsigned.

Later, the president asked Meade, "Do you know, General, what your attitude towards Lee after the battle of Gettysburg reminded me of?"

"No, Mr. President—what is it?"

"I'll be hanged if I could think of anything but an old woman trying to shoo her geese across the creek."[18]

The victories at Gettysburg, Vicksburg, and Port Hudson greatly cheered the North. The editor of *Harper's Weekly* exclaimed, "How marvelously the clouds seem to part! Three armies under three true and skillful leaders and upon three points successful! I think that for the first time we have a real confidence in our Generals."[19]

At the polls that fall, the public also expressed *real* confidence in Lincoln. George D. Morgan, brother of New York Governor Edwin D. Morgan, told a diplomat in Europe that the president "is very popular and good men on all sides seem to regard him as the man for the place, for they see what one cannot see abroad, how difficult the position he has to fill, to keep the border states quiet, to keep peace with the different Generals, and give any satisfaction to the radicals."[20] John Hay offered a more elaborate explanation of why Lincoln commanded respect. Writing from the White House to a friend, Hay said that the president "is in fine whack. I have rarely seen him more serene & busy. He is managing this war, the draft, foreign relations, and planning a reconstruction of the Union, all at once. . . . I am growing more and more firmly convinced that the good of the country absolutely demands that he should be kept where he is till this thing is over. There is no man in the country, so wise, so gentle and so firm. I believe the hand of God placed him where he is." Hay scoffed at reports that Radicals dominated the administration: "You may talk as you please of the Abolition Cabal directing affairs from Washington: some well meaning newspapers advise the President to keep his fingers out of the military pie: and all that sort of thing. The truth is, if he did, the pie would be a sorry mess. The old man sits here and wields like a backwoods Jupiter the bolts of war and the machinery of government with a hand equally steady & equally firm."[21]

The most important election that fall took place in Ohio, where Clement L. Vallandigham, one of Lincoln's most vehement critics, was running for governor. Vallandigham led the Peace Democrats, also known as Copperheads; they bitterly opposed emancipation and demanded that hostilities cease and that a compromise peace be negotiated. They also denounced the military draft, which Congress enacted in March 1863 and which began to be implemented soon thereafter.[22] Resistance to the draft was widespread, especially in New York City, where for three days in mid-July 1863, antidraft rioters ran amok, destroying draft offices and killing many blacks, among them some children.

Lincoln feared "the fire in the rear"—the Peace Democrats—more than he feared military defeat. When told that he faced problems like those that had confronted the French statesman Cardinal Richelieu, Lincoln replied, "Far from it, Richelieu never had a fire in his front and rear at the same time, as I have."[23]

Ohio Democrats nominated Vallandigham for governor after he had been arrested in May for denouncing the war effort. Following the Fredericksburg debacle, Lincoln had assigned General Ambrose E. Burnside to command the Army of the Ohio. In that capacity, the hapless general unwisely issued an order stating that "the habit of declaring sympathy for the enemy will not be allowed in this department. Persons committing such offenses will be at once arrested," tried by military courts "as spies or traitors, and, if convicted, will suffer death" or will be "sent beyond our lines into the lines of their friends."[24] In May 1863, Vallandigham ignored this draconian order and delivered a fiery speech that led to his arrest, trial, and imprisonment. Lincoln regretted the general's rash action that made Vallandigham a martyr. To mitigate the damage, Lincoln banished Vallandigham to the Confederacy. After spending a brief time in the South, Vallandigham went to Canada, where he campaigned in absentia for governor. The *New York Tribune* declared, "The fate of the Union rests upon the results of the election in Ohio."[25]

To help the Republican cause, Lincoln wrote an important public letter in which he defended both emancipation and the controversial decision to recruit black troops. Addressed to his Springfield friend James C. Conkling, who had invited him to speak at the Illinois capital, Lincoln's letter asked Peace Democrats some pointed questions: "You desire peace; and you blame me that we do not have it. But how can we attain it? There are but three conceivable ways. First, to suppress the rebellion by force of arms. This, I am trying to do. Are you for it? If you are, so far we are agreed. If you are not for it, a second way is, to give up the Union. I am against this. Are you for it? If you are, you should say so plainly. If you are not for *force*, nor yet for *dissolution*, there only remains some imaginable *compromise*." But, Lincoln insisted, no compromise restoring the Union could be negotiated, for neither the Confederate civilian nor military leadership was willing to accept such terms: "In an effort at such compromise we should waste time, which the enemy would improve to our disadvantage; and that would be all." Lincoln tackled the race issue head-on, challenging the Peace Democrats: "you are dissatisfied with me about the negro. Quite likely there is a difference of opinion between you and myself upon that subject. I certainly wish that all men could be free, while I suppose you do not." Lincoln said that he had issued the Emancipation Proclamation and had approved the recruitment of black troops as Union-saving measures. Military leaders, Lincoln pointed out, considered both of those steps essential to the war effort: "some of the commanders of our armies in the field who have given us our most important successes, believe the emancipation policy and the use of the colored troops the heaviest blow yet dealt to the rebellion."[26]

In an eloquent conclusion, Lincoln reflected on the significance of the war: "Peace does not appear so distant as it did. I hope it will come soon, and come to stay; and so come as to be worth the keeping in all future time. It will then have been proved that, among free men, there can be no successful appeal from the ballot to the bullet; and that they who take such appeal are sure to lose their case, and pay the cost." With crushing force he put critics of black recruitment in their place: "And then, there will be some black men who can remember that, with silent tongue, and clenched teeth, and steady eye, and well-poised bayonet, they have helped mankind on to this great consummation; while, I fear, there will be some white ones, unable to forget that, with malignant heart, and deceitful speech, they have strove to hinder it."[27]

Widely circulated as a campaign document, this powerful letter helped Republicans to triumph not only in Ohio (where Vallandigham was soundly defeated) but also in other states, most crucially Pennsylvania. In the Keystone State, the incumbent Republican governor, Andrew G. Curtin, narrowly won reelection over his Democratic opponent, who had been publicly endorsed by General McClellan. The governor of Maine declared that the Conkling letter "aided not a little in swelling our wonderful majority" in the fall election.[28]

Charles Eliot Norton, a Massachusetts intellectual who had earlier criticized Lincoln's rhetoric, lauded "the extraordinary excellence of the President's letter." Norton thought that Lincoln rose "with each new effort, and his letters are successive victories." The public letters "are, as he says to General Grant of Vicksburg, 'of almost inestimable value to the country,'—for they are of the rarest class of political documents, arguments seriously addressed by one in power to the conscience and reason of the citizens of the commonwealth." Such public letters, Norton concluded, were "examples of the possibility of the coexistence of a strong government with entire and immediate dependence upon and direct appeal to the people. There is in them the clearest tone of uprightness of character, purity of intention, and goodness of heart."[29]

The Republicans won handily despite a military setback in September, when William S. Rosecrans suffered the only major loss that the Union armies sustained in the West. (In effect, the war was won in the West, while Union forces in the East fought the Confederates to a draw.) Rosecrans had skillfully maneuvered Braxton Bragg out of Chattanooga, Tennessee, but had incautiously pursued him into Georgia, where Bragg turned and whipped him at the Battle of Chickamauga. The Army of the Cumberland was driven back into Chattanooga, which Bragg besieged.

To save Rosecrans, Lincoln authorized the most successful and dramatic use of railroads in the war. With Stanton overseeing the operation, trains whisked twenty-three thousand men under Hooker from Virginia to Chattanooga. Their arrival staved off immediate defeat, but it was not clear that Union forces could survive the siege. Rosecrans's erratic behavior worried Lincoln, who said that the general seemed "confused and stunned like a duck hit on the head."[30] So the president put Grant in charge of all western armies and authorized him to replace Rosecrans. Grant did so, naming as Old Rosy's successor George H. Thomas, who had kept the Union defeat at Chickamauga from becoming a complete rout. Apropos of Thomas's achievement, which earned him the sobriquet "the Rock of Chickamauga," Lincoln said, "It is doubtful whether his heroism and skill . . . has ever been surpassed in the world."[31] In November 1863, Grant, with the assistance of Thomas and Hooker, thrashed Bragg at the Battle of Chattanooga. Grant's triumph led to his appointment, three months later, as commander of all Union armies.

On the heels of the victory at Chattanooga—coming on top of victories at Gettysburg, Vicksburg, and Port Hudson—Lincoln evidently thought that reasonable Southerners would acknowledge the impossibility of winning independence through continued fighting and would therefore be inclined to surrender if they were offered generous peace terms. So in December 1863, he proposed a Reconstruction plan whereby most Confederates would receive pardon and amnesty if they merely took an oath of future loyalty to the United States. Once a certain number of voters in a Confederate state took that oath (a number equal to 10 percent of those who had cast ballots in the 1860 election), the state could once again enjoy full-fledged membership in the Union, provided only that it accepted the abolition of slavery. (Confederates not eligible for blanket amnesty were military and civilian leaders, men who resigned commissions in the U.S. Army or Navy or a post in the federal government, or men who mistreated captured black troops or their white officers.)

Lincoln spelled out his new Reconstruction policy in a proclamation attached to his 1863 annual message to Congress, which emphasized his commitment to emancipation. Any backsliding, he insisted, "would also be a cruel and astounding breach of faith." As long as he was president, Lincoln asserted, "I shall not attempt to retract or modify the emancipation proclamation; nor shall I return to slavery any person who is free by the terms of that proclamation, or by any of the acts of Congress." Lincoln indicated that he was flexible on Reconstruction policy: "Saying that, on certain terms, certain classes will be pardoned, with rights restored, it is not said that other classes, or other terms, will never be included. Saying that reconstruction will be accepted if presented in a specified way, it is not said it will never be accepted in any other way."[32] It is hard to know exactly what Lincoln had in mind by stressing his flexibility, but he may well have been paving the way for black suffrage. As it stood, the so-called Ten Percent Plan had nothing to say about black citizenship rights.

The most promising state for early restoration was Louisiana, where an election was held in February 1864. Voters there chose as their governor Michael Hahn, to whom Lincoln suggested in March 1864 that the new constitution that Louisianans would soon adopt should provide for limited black voting rights: "Now you are about to have a Convention which, among other things, will probably define the elective franchise. I barely suggest for your private consideration, whether some of the colored people may not be let in—as, for instance, the very intelligent, and especially those who have fought gallantly in our ranks. They would probably help, in some trying time to come, to keep the jewel of liberty within the family of freedom."[33]

Lincoln's suggestion to Governor Hahn may have resulted from a recent White House visit by a delegation of New Orleans free blacks, who had submitted to him a petition signed by one thousand blacks who wanted to vote. The delegation was led by Jean Baptiste Roudeanez and Arnold Bertonneau, who informed the president that twenty-nine thousand of Louisiana's thirty thousand free blacks were literate; that the free black community was taxed on property valued at more than $15,000,000; that many free blacks could trace their ancestry to French and Spanish settlers and to men who had fought alongside Andrew Jackson at the battle of New Orleans on January 8, 1815; that many free blacks had lighter skins than some whites; and that free blacks had rallied to protect the Crescent City from a threatened Confederate attack while Banks was besieging Port Hudson. "We are men; treat us as such," they said.[34]

Lincoln may also have been inclined to support limited black suffrage after meeting with the nation's leading black abolitionist, Frederick Douglass, in August 1863. Douglass called at the White House to protest against the discrimination that black soldiers endured in both pay and promotions. (They were not allowed to become officers, nor did they receive the same wages as white troops.) Douglass reported that he was "received cordially" by Lincoln. "I have never seen a more transparent countenance, " Douglass wrote two days after the interview. "There was not the slightest shadow of embarrassment." Douglass felt "quite at home in his presence." Lincoln, he said, proceeded with "an earnestness and fluency of which I had not suspected him, to vindicate his policy respecting the whole slavery question and especially that in reference to employing colored troops." The president defended himself against some critics, like Ohio Senator John Sherman: "I have been charged with vacillation . . . but I think the charge cannot be sustained. No man can say that having once taken the position I have contradicted it or retreated from it." Douglass took this as "an assurance that whoever else might abandon his antislavery policy President Lincoln would stand firm to his." In explaining his delay in authorizing the enlistment of black troops, Lincoln (according to Douglass) "said that the country needed talking up to that point. He hesitated in regard to it when he felt that the country was not ready for it. He knew that the colored man throughout this country was a despised man, a hated man, and he knew that if he at first came out with such a proclamation, all the hatred which is poured on the head of the negro race would be visited on his Administration. He said that there was preparatory work needed, and that that preparatory work had been done." He described that "preparatory work" accomplished by heroic black troops earlier that summer at Fort Wagner, near Charleston, South Carolina, and at Port Hudson and Milliken's Bend, Louisiana: "Remember this, Mr. Douglass; remember that Milliken's Bend, Port Hudson, and Fort Wagner are recent events; and that these were necessary to prepare the way for this very proclamation of mine." If it had been issued earlier, he said, "such was the state of public popular prejudice that an outcry would have been raised against the measure. It would be said 'Ah! We thought it would come to this. White men are to be killed for negroes.'" Douglass thought this argument was "reasonable." In a letter recounting this meeting, he wrote, "My whole interview with the President was gratifying and did much to assure me that slavery would not survive the War and that the country would survive both slavery and the War."[35]

Lincoln would later say to Douglass, "There is no man's opinion that I value more than yours," and the president once told a friend "that considering the conditions from which Douglass rose, and the position to which he had attained he was, in his judgment, one of the most meritorious men in America."[36] Such men, Lincoln probably thought, deserve citizenship rights.

At first, Congress expressed approval of Lincoln's Reconstruction plan, but soon it grew suspicious. In July 1864, it passed a bill framed by two Radicals, Senator Benjamin F. Wade and Congressman Henry Winter Davis, offering a different approach to Reconstruction. It provided that when fighting came to an end within a state, a provisional governor, to be chosen by the president, would enroll adult white males (no blacks were permitted to vote) and ask them to swear an oath of allegiance to the Constitution. Once a majority of those men (not the mere 10 percent called for in Lincoln's plan) had taken the oath, an election would be held for delegates to a constitutional convention. Only men who took an "iron-clad" oath that they had never fought against the Union were eligible to serve as delegates to the constitutional conventions or to vote in the subsequent ratification contests. Those new constitutions had to abolish slavery, repudiate all debts incurred during the war, and bar from voting and office holding any leading member of the Confederate military or civilian government. By requiring that a *majority* had to take the ironclad oath, the Wade-Davis bill guaranteed that Reconstruction would be undertaken entirely after the war; Lincoln desired to implement Reconstruction while the fighting continued in order to help induce the Confederates to surrender. The congressional insistence on a retrospective oath dismayed Lincoln, who objected to any oath "which requires a man to swear he has not done wrong" because it "rejects the Christian principle of forgiveness on terms of repentance. I think it is enough if the man does no wrong *hereafter*."[37]

The failure of the Wade-Davis statute to enfranchise blacks disappointed some Radicals but not New Hampshire Senator John P. Hale, who said he disagreed "with those who hold that the right of voting is a right which belongs to the catalogue of a man's natural rights & that it is quite as wrong to withhold that from him [the black man] as it is to keep him in a state of bondage. That is not so, it is not a natural right but a political one bestowed by those who frame the political institutions of a Country. If it were a natural right it would belong to women as well as to man [*sic*], & society in forming its institutions and organizations has a right to with-hold it from any person or class of persons who it believes cannot exercise it understandingly & in a manner that will subserve and promote the best interests of society."[38] (Lincoln, as noted above, was then working behind the scenes to cajole Louisiana whites into allowing at least some blacks to vote.)

In July 1864, Lincoln pocket vetoed the Wade-Davis Bill, much to the dismay of its authors. Davis excoriated Lincoln bitterly. A fellow Maryland Radical exclaimed that the self-righteous, vain, and impulsive Davis "lives on wormwood & gall and aloes!"[39] With his customary magnanimity, Lincoln said of Davis's attack on him, "[I]t appears to do him good, and as it does me no injury, (that is I don't feel that it does) what's the harm in letting him have his fling? If he did not pitch into me he would into some poor fellow whom he might hurt."[40]

REELECTION

Congressman Henry Winter Davis and other Radicals vowed to defeat Lincoln for reelection. At first they had been attracted to the potential candidacy of Salmon P. Chase, who had long been scheming to win the Republican presidential nomination. Chase's head, Lincoln remarked, was "full of Presidential *maggots*," and while the president was "trying to keep the maggot out of his brain," he was "much amused" at the treasury secretary's "mad hunt after the Presidency."[1] Informed that Chase often criticized him behind his back, Lincoln replied that such criticism did not bother him, for the secretary was "on the whole, a pretty good fellow and a very able man" whose "only trouble is that he has 'the White House fever.'"[2] Therefore, Lincoln said, he "shut his eyes to all these performances." If Chase ever became president, Lincoln said it would be "all right. I hope we may never have a worse man." Lincoln thought Chase's ambition resembled "a horsefly on the neck of a ploughhorse—which kept him lively about his work."[3]

Lincoln's willingness to tolerate Chase's machinations was yet another example of his preternatural magnanimity. In February 1864, the president ignored Chase's backers who issued public calls for the Republican party to dump Lincoln in favor of their hero. When Chase disingenuously insisted that he had nothing to do with such pronouncements, Lincoln replied that he had not read the documents and that he wished the secretary to remain in the cabinet.[4] The president explained to another cabinet member that he believed

Chase's denial, "for he thought it impossible for him (Mr. Chase) to have done such a thing."[5]

"I do not meddle in these matters," Lincoln insisted. "If any man thinks my present position desirable to occupy, he is welcome to try it, as far as I am concerned."[6] Impressed by Lincoln's superhuman forbearance, U.S. Supreme Court Justice David Davis remarked that the president "is a wise man, & he won[']t quarrel with Chase. I w[oul]d dismiss him [from] the cabinet, if it killed me. He pursues the wiser course."[7] Another Supreme Court Justice, Noah H. Swayne, believed that if Lincoln "were not the self denigrating & most magnanimous man that he is there would be an explosion."[8]

An explosion did come, however, in June when Chase submitted his resignation. The secretary had bullied Lincoln with resignation threats on earlier occasions, and the president had backed down every time. Finally, Lincoln's almost infinite patience was exhausted. He told John Hay, "Mr. Chase has resigned and I have accepted his resignation. I thought I could not stand it any longer."[9]

Lincoln was clearly tired of Chase's attempts to dominate the administration. When the governor of Ohio volunteered to facilitate a reconciliation, Lincoln replied, "This is the third time he has thrown this [resignation] at me, and I do not think I am called to continue to beg him to take it back, especially when the country would not go to destruction in consequence."[10]

Moreover, the president did not like Chase personally, though he admired the secretary's ability and commitment to emancipation. (Lincoln disliked some other Radicals, less because of their politics than because of their style. While he shared their strong antislavery views and their desire to see the war prosecuted vigorously, Lincoln objected to what he called "the self-righteousness of the Abolitionists" and "the petulant and vicious fretfulness of many radicals.")[11]

Hay thought that the rupture was caused by Chase's voracious appetite for deference, even from the president: it was Lincoln's "intellectual arrogance and unconscious assumption of superiority" that Chase "could never forgive."[12] Hay's analysis is only partly true. Lincoln was not "intellectually arrogant," but beneath his self-abnegating persona, he had a deep-rooted sense of self that gave him dignity, strength, and confidence.

Many foes of slavery found Chase objectionable because, as General Rutherford B. Hayes of Ohio remarked, he was "cold, selfish, and unscrupulous." Hayes believed that "political intrigue, love of power, and a selfish and boundless ambition were the striking features of his life and character."[13] A Philadelphia abolitionist deemed Chase "[b]ig-brained, cold-hearted, selfish, suspicious and parsimonious."[14]

Hay was right when he insisted that "the President has made a mistake" by accepting Chase's resignation, especially since he nominated an unimpressive man, former Ohio Governor David Tod, to replace the treasury secretary. Illinois Congressman Elihu Washburne told his old friend Lincoln that it was "a great disaster: At this time, ruinous; that time of military unsuccess, financial weakness, Congressional hesitation on the question of conscription & imminent famine in the West."[15] (When Tod sensibly withdrew his name from consideration, Lincoln redeemed himself by appointing William P. Fessenden, chairman of the Senate Finance Committee, as Chase's successor.)

Washburne was wrong about the famine but right about the lack of military success. In March 1864, when Lincoln named Ulysses S. Grant commander of all Union armies, the public understandably expected that the Hero of Fort Henry, Fort Donelson, Shiloh, Vicksburg, and Chattanooga would conquer the Confederacy in short order. In consultation with Lincoln, the general had devised a masterful spring offensive. Under George Gordon Meade (accompanied by Grant), the Army of the Potomac would march overland toward Richmond; under Benjamin F. Butler, another army would move west on Richmond from the peninsula; yet another army would sweep the Shenandoah Valley; in the west, William T. Sherman would march on Atlanta; N. P. Banks would move against Confederate forces in Louisiana; and the navy under David Farragut would seize control of Mobile Bay, Alabama. The coordinated assaults should bring the Confederacy to its knees by midsummer.

But it did not. Robert E. Lee bloodied the Army of the Potomac badly in a series of battles in May and June, inflicting enormous casualties. Instead of capturing Richmond, Union forces under Meade and Grant found themselves bogged down in a siege of Petersburg, twenty miles south of the Confederate capital. Union advances on the peninsula and in the Shenandoah Valley were stymied. Banks's Red River campaign was a fiasco. Sherman's progress toward Atlanta was agonizingly slow. By July, Northern public opinion had turned against the Lincoln administration as spring optimism gave way to summer despair.

In early June, Republicans renominated Lincoln, but within weeks, many of them came to have buyers' remorse. Radicals launched movements to dump him from the ticket. Various alternative candidates were considered, foremost among them John C. Frémont, the party's standard bearer in 1856, and Butler, a leading Massachusetts Radical. Both men were generals who had demonstrated abundant military ineptitude but had endeared themselves to Radicals with their antislavery actions. In May, when John Hay stated, "Butler was the only man in the army in whom power would be dangerous," Lincoln replied, "Yes, he is like Jim Jett's brother. Jim used to say that his brother was the dam[n]dest scoundrel that ever lived but in the infinite mercy of Providence he was also the dam[n]dest fool."[16] Butler was not foolish enough to challenge Lincoln for the nomination.

Frémont, however, was. In late May, disaffected Radicals gathered in Cleveland and nominated him for president. When told that only four hundred delegates had attended that conclave, Lincoln reached for his Bible and read aloud a passage about the supporters of David at the cave of Adullam: "And every one that was in distress, and every one that was in debt, and every one that was discontented, gathered themselves unto him, and he became a captain over them, and there were with him about four hundred men."[17]

Those delegates adopted a platform calling for a constitutional amendment abolishing slavery throughout the nation. Lincoln urged the Republican convention to follow suit, which it did the following week.

Frémont's acceptance letter, which sounded more like the handiwork of a Copperhead foe of Lincoln rather than a militant foe of slavery, disappointed many Radicals but not Lincoln's most vehement abolitionist critic, Wendell Phillips. In a letter to the Cleveland convention, that celebrated Boston orator denounced the administration as "a civil and military failure" and predicted that if the president won reelection, "I do not expect to see the Union reconstructed in my day, unless on terms more disastrous to liberty than even Disunion would be." Lincoln's Reconstruction policy "makes the freedom of the negro a sham," "perpetuates slavery under a softer name," and "puts all power into the hands of the unchanged white race, soured by defeat, hating the laboring class, plotting constantly for aristocratic institutions." Phillips lauded Frémont, "whose first act was to use the freedom of the negro as his weapon . . . whose thorough loyalty to democratic institutions, without regard to race—whose earnest and decisive character, whose clear-sighted statesmanship and rare military ability, justify my confidence that in his hands all will be done to save the state that foresight, skill, decision and statesmanship can do."[18]

Many Radicals demurred, including the nation's most prominent abolitionist, William Lloyd Garrison, editor of the *Liberator*. Garrison called Lincoln's reelection essential for "the suppression of the rebellion, and the abolition of slavery." He conceded that the president was "open to criticism and censure" but insisted that there "is also much to rejoice over and to be thankful for; and a thousand incidental errors and blunders are easily to be borne with on the part of one who, at one blow, severed the chains of three millions three hundred thousand slaves,—thus virtually abolishing the whole slave system . . . as an act dictated alike the patriotism, justice and humanity."[19] Garrison urged his fellow abolitionists to understand that Lincoln's "freedom to follow his convictions of duty as an individual is one thing—as the President of the United States, it is limited by the functions of his office; for the people do not elect a President to play the part of reformer or philanthropist, nor to enforce upon the nation his own peculiar ethical or humanity ideas, without regard to his oath or their will. His primary and all-comprehensive duty is to maintain the Union and execute the Constitution, in good faith . . . without reference to the views of any clique or party in the land." Garrison was firmly convinced that "no man has occupied the chair of the Chief Magistracy in America, who has more assiduously or more honestly endeavored to discharge all its duties with a single eye to the welfare of the country, than Mr. Lincoln."[20] In September, Garrison told a guest, "I have every confidence in Mr. Lincoln's honesty; his honor is involved in his fidelity to the Emancipation Proclamation."[21]

To a British scoffer, Garrison conceded that Lincoln "might have done more and gone further, if he had had greater resolution and larger foresight; that is an open question, and opinions are not facts. Possibly he could not have gone one hair's breadth beyond the point he has reached by a slow and painful process, without inciting civil war at the North, and overturning the government." Insisting that such speculation was "idle," Garrison focused on what was known about Lincoln's record: "that his Emancipation proclamation of January 1, 1863, liberated more than three-fourths of the entire slave population; that since that period, emancipation has followed in Maryland, Western Virginia, Missouri, and the District of Columbia, and is being rapidly consummated in Kentucky and Tennessee, thus terminating the holding of property in man everywhere under the American flag; that all the vast Territories have been consecrated to freedom and free labor; that all Fugitive Slave laws have been repealed, so that slave-hunting is at an end in all the free States; that no rebel State can be admitted to the Union, except on the basis of complete emancipation; that national justice (refused under every other Administration) has been done to the republics of Hayti and Liberia, by the full recognition of their independence; that an equitable treaty has been made with Great Britain for the effectual suppression of the foreign slave trade, through right of search; that a large portion of the army is made up of those who, until now, have been prohibited bearing arms, and refused enrolment in the militia of every State in the Union [i.e., black men]; . . . that free negro schools are following wherever the army penetrates, and multitudes of young and old, who, under the old slave system, were prohibited learning the alphabet, are now rapidly acquiring that knowledge which is power, and which makes slavery and serfdom alike impracticable; and that on numerous plantations free labor is 'in the full tide of successful experiment.'"[22]

A leading congressional Radical, Owen Lovejoy, told Garrison that Lincoln might not be "the best conceivable President," but he was "the best possible. I have known something of the facts inside during his administration, and I know that he has been just as radical as any of his Cabinet. And although he does not do everything that you or I would like, the question recurs, whether it is likely we can elect a man who would."[23] Lovejoy thought it "impolitic, not to say cruel, to sharply criticize even the mistakes of an executive weighed down and surrounded with cares and perplexities, such as have fallen to but few of those upon whom have been laid the affairs of Government." Lovejoy begged his fellow Radicals, "Do not let any power from earth or from beneath the earth alienate your attachment or weaken your confidence in the President. He has given us the Proclamation of Freedom. He has solemnly declared he will not revoke it. And although he may seem to lead the Isaac of freedom bound to the altar, you may rest assured that it is done from a conviction of duty, and that the sacrificial knife will never fall on the lad."[24] Radical critics of Lincoln should realize that he "is at heart as strong an anti-slavery man as any of them," but he "has a responsibility in this matter which many men do not seem to be able to comprehend." Lovejoy acknowledged that the president's "mind works slowly" but insisted that "when he moves, it is *forward*."[25]

The military stalemate led many Northerners to lose heart and call for peace. In July, Horace Greeley told Lincoln that "our bleeding, bankrupt, almost dying country . . . longs for peace" and "shudders at the prospect of fresh conscriptions, of further wholesale devastations, and of new rivers of human blood."[26] When Confederate emissaries in Canada suggested to Greeley that peace might be obtained through negotiations, that influential editor urged Lincoln to explore the possibility. (Lincoln said Greeley "means right" but "makes me almost as much trouble as the whole southern confederacy.")[27] Unwilling to seem intransigent, the president suggested that Greeley himself deal with those agents. Reluctantly, Greeley traveled to Niagara Falls and met the Confederates. When he discovered that those gentlemen were not in fact authorized to negotiate on behalf of the Jefferson Davis government, he asked for instructions from Lincoln, who replied, "Any proposition which embraces the restoration of peace, the integrity of the whole Union, and the abandonment of slavery, and which comes by and with an authority that can control the armies now at war against the United States will be received and considered by the Executive government of the United States, and will be met by liberal terms on other substantial and collateral points, and the bearer or bearers thereof shall have safe conduct both ways."[28]

Democrats denounced this "Niagara Manifesto," charging that Lincoln was turning a war to save the Union into an antislavery crusade. They called the Niagara Manifesto "a *finality*, which . . . will preclude any conference for a settlement. Every soldier . . . that is killed, will lose his life not for the Union, the Stars and Stripes, but for the negro."[29] The *Detroit Free Press* argued that the manifesto showed how Lincoln was "bound hand and foot to the dogmas of the extreme abolitionists."[30] Other Democratic newspapers called it evidence that "our flippant, cunning undignified despot" was prosecuting the war to "liberate the negro and rivet their chains upon white freemen."[31]

Republicans worried about the manifesto's political effects. One called the document a "blunder" by Lincoln that "may cost him his election. By declaring that abandonment of slavery is a fundamental article in any negotiation for peace and settlement, he has given the disaffected and discontented a weapon that doubles their power of mischief."[32]

As the summer wore on and Republican prospects grew ever bleaker, Lincoln came under increasing pressure to repudiate the Niagara Manifesto. The president replied to those urging such a step, "[T]here has never been a time since the war began when I was not willing to stop it if I could do so and preserve the Union, and earlier in the war I would have omitted some of the conditions of my note to the rebel Commissioners, but I had become satisfied that no lasting peace could be built up between the States in some of which there were free and in others slave institutions, and, therefore, I made the recognition of the abolition of slavery a *sine qua non*."[33] More emphatically, he told a visitor in late August, "There have been men who have proposed to me to return to slavery the black warriors of Port Hudson & Olustee to their masters to conciliate the South. I should be damned in time & in eternity for so doing. The world shall know that I will keep my faith to friends & enemies, come what will.

My enemies say I am now carrying on this war for the sole purpose of abolition. It is & will be carried on so long as I am President for the sole purpose of restoring the Union. But no human power can subdue this rebellion without using the Emancipation lever as I have done. Freedom has given us the control of 200,000 able bodied men, born & raised on southern soil. It will give us more yet. Just so much it has sub[t]racted from the strength of our enemies, & instead of alienating the south from us, there are evidences of a fraternal feeling growing up between our own & rebel soldiers. My enemies condemn my emancipation policy. Let them prove by the history of this war, that we can restore the Union without it."[34]

And yet Lincoln did toy with the idea of backing away from the Niagara Manifesto. In mid-August, he drafted a letter to a War Democrat who had criticized it.[35] In that missive, the president appeared to renege on the demand that abolition be made a prerequisite for peace. He wrote that "saying re-union and abandonment of slavery would be considered, if offered, is not saying that nothing *else* or *less* would be considered, if offered." He noted that "no one, having control of the rebel armies, or, in fact, having any influence whatever in the rebellion, has offered, or intimated a willingness to, a restoration of the Union, in any event, or on any condition whatever. . . . If Jefferson Davis wishes, for himself, or for the benefit of his friends at the North, to know what I would do if he were to offer peace and re-union, saying nothing about slavery, let him try me."[36] When Frederick Douglass urged him not to send that letter, Lincoln agreed.

Douglass had come to the White House at Lincoln's request to discuss the election. The president, fearing that a Democrat would be chosen president, told his guest that "slaves are not coming so rapidly and so numerously to us as I had hoped." (The situation had changed since 1862, when Lincoln had informed his friend Orville H. Browning that the flood of escaped slaves posed a significant problem.) Douglass "replied that the slaveholders knew how to keep such things from their slaves, and probably very few knew of his Proclamation." Lincoln suggested "that something should be speedily done to inform the slaves in the Rebel states of the true state of affairs in relation to them" and "to warn them as to what will be their probable condition should peace be concluded while they remain within the Rebel lines: and more especially to urge upon them the necessity of making their escape." Douglass recalled that Lincoln's words "showed a deeper moral conviction against slavery than I had even seen before in anything spoken or written by him." The president said, "Douglass, I hate slavery as much as you do, and I want to see it abolished altogether."[37] (The black orator agreed to help organize an effort to recruit a band of black scouts "whose business should be somewhat after the original plan of John Brown, to go into the rebel states, beyond the lines of our armies, and carry the news of emancipation, and urge the slaves to come within our boundaries.")[38] Lincoln's appeal to Douglass casts doubt on the theory that the slaves liberated themselves and that Lincoln had precious little to do with emancipation.[39]

Lincoln took another step in anticipation of a Democratic victory. On August 23, he wrote a memorandum that he did not read to his cabinet but which he asked each member to sign: "This morning, as for some days past, it seems exceedingly probable that this Administration will not be re-elected. Then it will be my duty to so co-operate with the President elect, as to save the Union between the election and the inauguration; as he will have secured his election on such ground that he can not possibly save it afterwards."[40]

Months later, Lincoln read this "blind memorandum" to the cabinet and explained its origin: "[Y]ou will remember that this was written at a time (6 days before the Chicago [Democratic party] nominating convention) when as yet we had no adversary, and seemed to have no friends. I then solemnly resolved on the course of action indicated above. I resolved, in case of the election of General Mc-Clellan[,] being certain that he would be the Candidate, that I would see him and talk matters over with him. I would say, 'General, the election has demonstrated that you are stronger, have more influence with the American people than I. Now let us together, you with your influence and I with all the executive power of the Government, try to save the country. You raise as many troops as you possibly can for this final trial, and I will devote all my energies to assisting and finishing the war.'" Seward sneered, "And the General would answer you

'*Yes, Yes*'; and the next day when you saw him again & pressed these views upon him he would say, 'Yes—yes' & so on forever and would have done nothing at all." "At least," Lincoln responded, "I should have done my duty and have stood clear before my own conscience."[41]

Because it seemed that Lincoln had no chance of reelection, some Republicans dreamed of replacing him at the head of the ticket. But on August 25, an influential Massachusetts industrialist, John Murray Forbes, warned that it was too late. "We cannot change our Candidate," he wrote. If the Peace Democrats "keep in the background & let the opposition put up some one at Chicago who can catch the votes of the war & peace opposition men[,] we shall have a hard time in electing Lincoln. Were we free today we could nominate [John A.] Dix or [Benjamin F.] Butler and elect him by a strong vote." But the time for such maneuvering had passed.[42]

Instead of naming a new candidate, some malcontents, led by Wendell Phillips, rallied around Frémont. Phillips wrote privately, "I would cut off my right hand before doing anything to aid A. L.'s election. I wholly distrust his fitness to settle this thing—indeed his purpose."[43] At Boston in October, he publicly excoriated Lincoln's "halting, half-way course, neither hot nor cold, wanting to save the North without hurting the South." That course was dictated not "from want of brains, but want of purpose, of willingness to strike home. Observe how tender the President has been towards the South, how unduly and dangerously reluctant he has been to approach the negro and use his aid. Vigorous, despotic, decisive everywhere else, he halts, hesitates, delays to hurt the South or help the negro." Phillips defiantly announced, "I mean to agitate till I bayonet him and his party into justice."[44] ("We must *bully* the Govt!" he insisted.)[45] At New York, Phillips denounced the administration's lack of "vigor," "will," "purpose," and "loyalty in the highest sense of the word" and accused Lincoln of "an undue tenderness toward the South, and an undue and dangerous reluctance to do justice to the negro." Moreover, Phillips maintained, Lincoln tyrannically violated the liberties of the people.

Phillips's pronouncements alienated many antislavery militants. Garrison criticized Phillips's Boston speech: "We cannot allow it to pass without expressing our regret to perceive what seems to us a set purpose—*prima facie*—to represent Mr. Lincoln in the worst possible light, to attribute to him the worst possible motives, to hold him up as an imbecile and a despot, and to damage his chance of re-election to the utmost extent."[46] Similarly, Garrison's son Wendell bemoaned the tendency of Phillips and his followers "to distrust everybody, to endeavor by every ingenious device to find evidence that the government is the enemy of the black man & every officer under it unworthy to be trusted." He disapproved of their "[c]austic criticism, snap judgments, & wholesale asseveration" as well as their habit of having "only eyes for the shadows of the night & do not see the flood of daylight which is driving the blackness away."[47] In late August, a Radical ally told Phillips, "I came up [to New Hampshire] from Boston last night, sick at heart. Almost every abolitionist I see now, swears by Lincoln, & denounces your course."[48] Pennsylvania Congressman William D. Kelley spoke for many of them when he said, "Abraham Lincoln is the wisest radical of us all."[49]

On August 29, the political tide began turning dramatically when the Democratic national convention met in Chicago. The delegates adopted a platform declaring that the war had been nothing more than "four years of failure" and demanding that "immediate efforts be made for a cessation of hostilities, with a view to an ultimate convention of the states, or other peaceable means, to the end that, at the earliest practicable moment, peace many be restored on the basis of the Federal Union of the States." This so-called Peace Plank alienated many Northerners who might otherwise have voted Democratic. Making matters worse, the convention chose George B. McClellan to head the ticket and a notorious Copperhead, Ohio Congressman George Pendleton, as his running mate. A New York critic of Lincoln spoke for many War Democrats when he said, "I admire McClellan & should vote for him but I cannot swallow Pendleton & that Chicago platform. I never could digest them. The dyspepsia that would follow such a banquet would torment me all my days."[50]

As if the results of the Chicago convention were not enough to sink the Democrats, immediately after it adjourned, Sherman took Atlanta and set the North to rejoicing manically. On September 3, the Wall Street attorney George Templeton Strong captured the public mood when he recorded in his diary: "Glorious news this morn-ing—*Atlanta taken at last*!!!" It was, Strong said, "(coming at this political crisis) the greatest event of the war."[51] Three days later, John Nicolay, Lincoln's principal White House secretary, speculated that the "Atlanta victory alone ought to win the Presidential contest for us."[52] He wrote that the "political situation has not been as hopeful for six months past as it is just now. There is a perfect revolution in feeling. Three weeks ago, our friends everywhere were despondent, almost to the point of giving up the contest in despair. Now they are hopeful, jubilant, hard at work and confident of success."[53]

Frémont, who had hoped that the Democrats might nominate him, decided to drop out of the race but only if Lincoln would agree to fire the most prominent conservative in his cabinet, Postmaster General Montgomery Blair. (A leading Radical, Senator Zachariah Chandler of Michigan, brokered the deal.) Reluctantly, the presi-dent agreed, and Blair stepped down gracefully. Frémont was not so graceful in his withdrawal letter: "In respect to Mr. Lincoln, I consider that his Administration has been politically, militarily, and financially a failure, and that its necessary continuance is a cause of regret for the country."[54]

Republicans closed ranks swiftly after the Democratic conven-tion. Douglass, who had signed the call for the conclave that had nominated Frémont, endorsed Lincoln. "When there was any shadow of a hope that a man of a more decided anti-slavery conviction and policy could be elected, I was not for Mr. Lincoln," he told a fellow abolitionist. "But as soon as the Chicago convention [adjourned], my mind was made up." In a public letter, Douglass stated that "all hesitation ought to cease, and every man who wishes well to the slave and to the country should at once rally with all the warmth and earnestness of his nature to the support of Abraham Lincoln." Douglass did not stump for Lincoln because, as he put it, "Republican committees do not wish to expose themselves to the charge of being the 'N[igge]r' party. The Negro is the deformed child, which is put out of the room when company comes."[55]

As usual, the Democrats played the race card during the election campaign, with heavy emphasis on interracial sex. Two journalists coined a neologism for an anti-Republican pamphlet, *Miscegenation: The Theory of the Blending of the Races, Applied to the American White Man and Negro*, which they published anonymously and sent to leading antislavery spokesmen. (The common term for *miscegenation* had been *amalgamation*.) The authors hoped to trap some gullible Republicans into endorsing interracial marriage, but almost none of them did. Democrats occasionally called Republicans "nigger fuggers."[56] When Lincoln was asked if he supported miscegenation, he answered, "That's a [D]emocratic mode of producing good Union men, & I don't propose to infringe the patent."[57]

Lincoln sometimes rebutted racist arguments with sarcasm. In August, a Pennsylvanian with an unsure grasp of English grammar wrote him, "Equal Rights & Justice to all white men in the United States forever. White men is in class number one & black men is in class number two & must be governed by white men forever."[58] Lincoln penned a reply over the signature of his secretary, John G. Nicolay: "The President has received yours of yesterday, and is kindly paying attention to it. As it is my business to assist him whenever I can, I will thank you to inform me, for his use, whether you are either a white man or black one, because in either case, you can not be regarded as an entirely impartial judge. It may be that you belong to a third or fourth class of *yellow* or *red* men, in which case the impartiality of your judgment would be more apparent."[59]

Democrats denounced the president as an "executive trifler," a "retailer of smutty stories," a "tyrant over men's thoughts, presses, letters, persons, and lives," "a miserable failure, a coarse filthy joker, a disgusting politician, a mean, cunning and cruel tyrant and the shame and disgrace of the nation."[60] The strongly proslavery Samuel F. B. Morse called Lincoln an "illiterate," "inhuman," "wicked," and "*irreligious*" president "without brains" and a "coarse, vulgar, unculti-vated man, an inventor or re-teller of stories so low and obscene, that no decent man can listen to them without disgust."[61] Hysterically one Democratic newspaper lamented "the threatened extinguishment of the experiment of free government," predicted that the fall elections might well be the last "to receive the votes of freeman," and declared that under "Abraham the First," the United States had become "the

Russia of the Western Hemisphere."[62] The former mayor of Cincinnati predicted that Lincoln and his party "will proclaim themselves in power during the war. . . . I believe that Lincoln will not give up the idea of accomplishing the great idea of the war, though he may be compelled to resort to the *levy en masse*."[63] In Ohio's capital, newspaper editor Samuel Medary asserted that "everybody not crazy with 'negro on the brain'" knows that "Lincoln is running our country to perdition—destroying 'life, liberty and the pursuit of happiness'" as he sought to make himself a king.[64]

Since they maintained that Lincoln was a tyrant bent on destroying free government, some Democratic newspapers recommended that he be killed. The *La Crosse (WI) Democrat* asserted that if Lincoln were reelected, someone should assassinate him: "The man who votes for Lincoln now is a traitor. Lincoln is a traitor and murderer. He who, pretending to war for, wars against the constitution of our country is a traitor, and Lincoln is one of those men. He who calls and allures men to certain butchery, is a murderer, and Lincoln has done all this. . . . And if he is elected to misgovern for another four years, we trust some bold hand will pierce his heart with dagger point for the public good."[65] The *Albany (NY) Atlas and Argus* paraphrased Patrick Henry's 1765 "treason" speech: "Caesar had his Brutus, Charles I his Cromwell . . . and we the People recommend Abraham Lincoln to profit by their example."[66] Less-bloody-minded Democrats urged that Lincoln be impeached rather than assassinated.

The Democrats' charge that Lincoln told off-color jokes was accurate. In the late spring of 1864, he regaled his good friends David Davis and Leonard Swett with a story "about a man and a woman in the old days traveling up and down the country with a fiddle and a banjo making music for their living. And the man was proud of his wife's virtue and was always saying that no man could get to her, and he would trust her with any man who wanted to try it on a bet. And he made a bet with a stranger one day and the stranger took the wife into a room while the husband stood outside the door and played his fiddle. For quite a while he stood there playing his fiddle, and at last sang a song to her asking her how she was coming along with the stranger. She replied with a song of her own:

> He's got me down,
> He's clasped me round the middle;
> Kiss my ass and go to hell;
> Be off with your damned old fiddle."

David Davis scolded Lincoln, "[I]f the country knew you were telling those stories, you could never be elected and you know it." In reply, the president merely laughed.[67]

Some ex-Whig friends of Lincoln in Illinois, like John Todd Stuart and Orville H. Browning, had grown disenchanted with him. "I am personally attached to the President, and have faithfully tried to uphold him, and make him respectable," Browning said, "tho' I never have been able to persuade myself that he was big enough for his position. Still, I thought he might get through, as many a boy has got through College, without disgrace, and without knowledge, but I fear he is a failure."[68] Browning nonetheless did vote and campaign for Lincoln, albeit without enthusiasm.

Democrats also assailed Lincoln's wife, alleging accurately that she had padded payrolls and expense accounts, had accepted bribes and kickbacks, had spent government funds recklessly, and had behaved outrageously in public. During the campaign, Mary Todd Lincoln persuaded lobbyists to give her money. She confided to her close friend Elizabeth Keckly, "I have an object in view, Lizabeth. In a political canvass it is policy to cultivate every element of strength. These men have influence, and we require influence to reelect Mr. Lincoln. I will be clever to them until after the election, and then, if we remain at the White House, I will drop every one of them, and let them know very plainly that I only made tools of them. They are an unprincipled set, and I don't mind a little double-dealing with them." When asked if her husband knew about those schemes, she replied, "God! No; he would never sanction such a proceeding, so I keep him in the dark, and will tell him of it when all is over. He is too honest to take proper care of his own interests, so I feel it to be my duty to electioneer for him."[69]

Mrs. Lincoln's spendthrift ways angered some Union soldiers. "I can hardly wish that Mrs. Lincoln should occupy the White House for four years longer," remarked a trooper who supported the president for reelection. "Her want of sympathy with the loyal ladies of the North—our mothers and sisters, who to their arduous labors in behalf of our soldiers in the field and in the hospitals, have added dispensing with expensive luxuries that our National finances may be thereby improved, is not at all to her credit."[70]

Mary Lincoln was terrified that her husband might lose the election. When a spiritualist predicted that Lincoln would be defeated, she returned to the White House "crying *like a child*."[71] There the president told her, "Mary, I am afraid you will be punished for this overweening anxiety. If I am to be re-elected, it will be all right; if not, you must bear the disappointment." Her anxiety was understandable, for she had incurred huge debts that creditors would call in if Lincoln lost. She again confided to Keckly, "I have contracted large debts of which he [Lincoln] knows nothing, and which he will be unable to pay if he is defeated." She identified them as "store bills," mainly from Alexander T. Stewart's glamorous New York emporium. "You understand, Lizabeth, that Mr. Lincoln has but little idea of the expense of a woman's wardrobe. He glances at my rich dresses, and is happy in the belief that the few hundred dollars that I obtain from him supply all my wants. The people scrutinize every article that I wear with critical curiosity. The very fact of having grown up in the West, subjects me to more searching observation. To keep up appearances, I must have money—more than Mr. Lincoln can spare for me. He is too honest to make a penny outside of his salary; consequently, I had, and still have, no alternative but to run in debt." She explained why she kept these expenses secret from Lincoln: "if he knew that his wife was involved to the extent that she is, the knowledge would drive him mad. He is so sincere and straightforward himself, that he is shocked by the duplicity of others. He does not know a thing about any debts, and I value his happiness, not to speak of my own, too much to allow him to know anything. This is what troubles me so much. If he is re-elected, I can keep him in ignorance of my affairs."[72]

Democrats also protested against the "shameful disregard of the Administration to its duty in respect to our fellow citizens who now are and long have been prisoners of war and in a suffering condition."[73] In fact, the suffering of prisoners of war on both sides was acute, but the blame rested primarily with the Confederates. At first, Lincoln had hesitated to negotiate any prisoner-exchange agreement lest he seem to acknowledge the legitimacy of the Confederate government. But in 1862, an exchange cartel was established that worked well for almost a year but collapsed when the Union began recruiting blacks, and the Confederates refused to exchange former slaves whom they captured in uniform. Secretary of War Edwin M. Stanton declared that any agreement to accept a discriminatory system of exchanges would be "a dishonor. . . . When [the Confederates] agree to exchange all alike there will be no difficulty."[74] In 1864, reports of Union prisoners' suffering at the notorious Andersonville prison in Georgia and elsewhere infuriated the Northerners, who demanded that something be done. But Lincoln rejected appeals for a prisoner exchange as long as the Rebels discriminated against black troops and their white officers. The Confederate government "excited the rage and disgust of Mr. Lincoln" when it forced black POWs to help build fortifications at Mobile, Alabama, instead of exchanging them.[75] The Democratic attempt to capitalize on the POW issue proved ineffective.

Equally ineffective was the Democrats' charge that Lincoln selfishly received his salary in gold while other government workers received greenbacks. The charge was effectively refuted by the Treasurer of the United States, who explained that the law required the president's salary to be paid in monthly warrant drafts, from which the recently enacted income tax was deducted. Often Lincoln let those drafts sit in his desk drawer for months at a time. When urged to cash those warrants and thereby gain hundreds of dollars in interest, Lincoln refused, "I reckon the Treasury needs it more than I do." Through his reluctance to cash his pay warrants, Lincoln contributed a net of $4,000 to the treasury.[76] The Democratic newspaper that made the charge angered Lincoln. "See to what depths of infamy a Northern Copperhead can descend," he said. "If the scoundrel who wrote that don't boil hereafter, it well be because the devil hasn't got iron enough to make gridirons."[77]

Republicans charged that the Democrats encouraged treasonous secret societies like the Sons of Liberty and Order of American Knights. Lincoln regarded such allegations skeptically, asserting that the Sons of Liberty was "a mere political organization, with about as much of malice and as much of puerility as the Knights of the Golden Circle." When Clement L. Vallandigham returned from Canada illegally to act as "Supreme Grand Commander" of the Sons of Liberty, Lincoln resisted advice to have him arrested. To John Hay, Lincoln stated "that the question for the Government to decide is whether it can afford to disregard the contempt of authority & breach of discipline displayed in Vallandigham's unauthorized return: for the rest, it cannot but result in benefit to the Union cause to have so violent and indiscreet a man go to Chicago [for the Democratic national convention] as a firebrand to his own party."[78]

Despite Lincoln's skepticism, there was in fact some truth in Republican charges about dangerous sedition, for Confederate agents did plot with Northern Democrats to free Rebel prisoners of war, to seize leading state officials, to foment uprisings on election day in Chicago and New York, and to encourage Midwestern states to secede.

Divisions within the Republican ranks posed the gravest threat to Lincoln's reelection chances. Nowhere was that problem more acute than in Missouri, where Radicals and Conservatives engaged in what Lincoln called "a pestilent factional quarrel among themselves." The strife was so intense because a true civil war raged within the state, where brother fought against brother, guerillas rampaged, and bushwhacking was widespread. The worst atrocity of the war against civilians was perpetrated in the summer of 1863, when Confederate guerilla chieftain William C. Quantrill led hundreds of Missourians on a raid against Lawrence, Kansas, where they killed over 180 men and boys in cold blood and torched many buildings. This act of terrorism shocked the North and led Missouri Radicals to demand that the general in charge there, John Schofield, be replaced.

The quarrel in Missouri constituted the greatest danger to Republican unity since the cabinet imbroglio following the Battle of Fredericksburg. Eyes throughout the North focused on the White House in September 1863, when a large delegation of Missouri and Kansas Radicals called at the White House. Led by the combative Charles D. Drake, they demanded the replacement of Schofield with a Radical like Ben Butler. Earlier, Drake had publicly called Lincoln a tyrant. In a long meeting with the delegation, the president said, "I am aware that by many, by some even among this delegation,—I shall not name them,— I have been in public speeches and in printed documents charged with 'tyranny' and willfulness, with a disposition to make my own personal will supreme. I do not intend to be a tyrant. At all events I shall take care that in my own eyes I do not become one. I shall always try and preserve one friend within me, whoever else fails me, to tell me that I have not been a tyrant, and that I have acted right. I have no right to act the tyrant to mere political opponents. If a man votes for supplies of men and money; encourages enlistments; discourages desertions; does all in his power to carry the war on to a successful issue,—I have no right to question him for his abstract political opinions. I must make a dividing line, somewhere between those who are the opponents of the Government and those who only oppose peculiar features of my administration while they sustain the Government."[79]

Later, Lincoln told John Hay that the Missouri Radicals "are nearer to me than the other side, in thought and sentiment, though bitterly hostile personally. They are utterly lawless—the unhandiest devils in the world to deal with—but after all their faces are set Zionwards."[80] He detected in the Radicals "the stuff which must save the state and on which we must mainly rely. They are absolutely uncorrosive by the virus of secession. It cannot touch or taint them." Their opponents, the Conservatives, on the other hand, "in casting about for votes to carry through their plans, are tempted to affiliate with those whose record is not clear. If one side must be crushed out & the other cherished there could be no doubt which side we would choose as fuller of hope for the future. We would have to side with the Radicals." But the Radicals' intolerance offended Lincoln: "They insist that I shall hold and treat Governor [Harrison] Gamble and his supporters—men appointed by loyal people of Mo. as reps. of Mo. loyalty—and who have done their whole duty in the war faithfully & promptly—who when they have disagreed with me have been silent and kept about the good work—that I shall treat these men as copperheads and enemies to the Govt. This is simply monstrous." Lincoln thought it ironic that some of the more vehement Radicals, like Drake, had once bitterly opposed abolition. Others had been Confederates. He did not object "to penitent rebels being radical: he was glad of it." But he believed that they should show more charity for Governor Gamble. In matters political, Lincoln said he "was in favor of short statutes of limitations."[81]

After perusing the protest of the Missouri and Kansas delegation, Lincoln wrote them, stating that when Unionists there disagreed about slavery, tempers were bound to flare: "[S]incerity is questioned, and motives are assailed. Actual war coming, blood grows hot, and blood is spilled. Thought is forced from old channels into confusion. Deception breeds and thrives. Confidence dies, and universal suspicion reigns. Each man feels an impulse to kill his neighbor, lest he be first killed by him. Revenge and retaliation follow. And all this, as before said, may be among honest men only. But this is not all. Every foul bird comes abroad, and every dirty reptile rises up. These add crime to confusion. Strong measures, deemed indispensable but harsh at best, such men make worse by mal-administration. Murders for old grudges, and murders for pelf, proceed under any cloak that will best cover for the oc[c]asion. These causes amply account for what has occurred in Missouri, without ascribing it to the weakness, or wickedness of any general."[82]

Lincoln managed to defuse the Missouri crisis by transferring Schofield to an active command under Sherman and sending Rosecrans to St. Louis as his replacement. But even so, when Missourians chose delegates to the 1864 Republican national convention, they sent two delegations. In keeping with Lincoln's instructions, the convention seated the Radicals and rejected the Conservatives. That delegation at first cast their ballots for Grant as the party's standard bearer, but then it moved to make Lincoln's nomination unanimous.

Divisions among New York's Republicans also worried Lincoln, for he had carried the state by only a narrow margin in 1860. He worked to compose the differences between the factions there, one headed by Greeley, the other by Seward and Thurlow Weed. The distribution of patronage was the main source of discord. Weed complained bitterly that the Greeley forces received an unfairly large share of the federal offices. To placate Lord Thurlow, Lincoln made several changes in the leadership of the New York Customs House and post office.

Lincoln failed to make all the changes that the pro-Seward politicos demanded. To one of them, who insisted that an official who opposed the president's renomination be fired, Lincoln replied, "You cannot think . . . [illegible] to be half as mean to me as I know him to be, but I can not run this thing upon the theory that every officeholder must think I am the greatest man in the nation, and I will not." The offending civil servant did not lose his job.[83] When an army officer was cashiered for giving a pro-McClellan speech, Lincoln rescinded the dismissal order. "Supporting McClellan for the presidency is no violation of military regulations," he remarked. "[A]s a question of taste of choosing between him and me, well, I'm the longest, but he's better looking."[84]

Lincoln also intervened to end bitter strife within the Pennsylvanian Republican ranks. There, Simon Cameron feuded with reformers, who regarded the former secretary of war as a spoilsman interested only in promoting his own political fortunes, not those of the party. In response to Lincoln's appeal, Cameron agreed to make peace with his critics and work hard for the national ticket. In the crucial October gubernatorial elections, Republicans barely managed to carry Pennsylvania but won handily in Ohio and Indiana.

Lincoln's uncanny ability to harmonize factions helped him win reelection. To a friend, he said, "I may not have made as great a President as some other men, but I believe I have kept these discordant elements together as well as anyone could."[85]

In keeping with the custom of the day, Lincoln did not overtly campaign for reelection, but he issued a public letter that helped the Republican cause. In April 1864, some Kentuckians had called on him to complain about his emancipation policies and the recruitment of black soldiers. After he defended his record, one of his visitors asked him to write out what he had told them. Lincoln obliged in a letter that was widely published. In it, he boldly asserted, "I am naturally anti-slavery. If slavery is not wrong, nothing is wrong. I can not remember when I did not so think, and feel." But he did not feel authorized to act on his antislavery feelings: "I have never understood that the Presidency conferred upon me an unrestricted right to act officially upon this judgment and feeling. It was in the oath I took that I would, to the best of my ability, preserve, protect, and defend the Constitution of the United States. I could not take the office without taking the oath. Nor was it my view that I might take an oath to get power, and break the oath in using the power. I understood, too, that in ordinary civil administration this oath even forbade me to practically indulge my primary abstract judgment on the moral question of slavery." Lincoln insisted, "I have done no official act in mere deference to my abstract judgment and feeling on slavery." But he could act against slavery if such action would help win the war: "I did understand however, that my oath to preserve the constitution to the best of my ability, imposed upon me the duty of preserving, by every indispensable means, that government—that nation—of which that constitution was the organic law. Was it possible to lose the nation, and yet preserve the constitution? By general law life and limb must be protected; yet often a limb must be amputated to save a life; but a life is never wisely given to save a limb. I felt that measures, otherwise unconstitutional, might become lawful, by becoming indispensable to the preservation of the constitution, through the preservation of the nation. Right or wrong, I assumed this ground, and now avow it. I could not feel that, to the best of my ability, I had even tried to preserve the constitution, if, to save slavery, or any minor matter, I should permit the wreck of government, country, and Constitution all together." Lincoln reminded the Kentuckians of his decision to override Frémont's emancipation order in 1861, of his similar treatment of General David Hunter the following year, of his insistence that Secretary of War Cameron withdraw his public recommendation that black men be recruited and armed, and of his repeated appeals to the Border States to accept his plan of gradual emancipation with compensation and colonization. After the failure of his third attempt to persuade the Border States, he had run out of patience: "They declined the proposition; and I was, in my best judgment, driven to the alternative of either surrendering the Union, and with it, the Constitution, or of laying strong hand upon the colored element. I chose the latter. In choosing it, I hoped for greater gain than loss; but of this, I was not entirely confident. More than a year of trial now shows no loss by it in our foreign relations, none in our home popular sentiment, none in our white military force,—no loss by it any how or any where. On the contrary, it shows a gain of quite a hundred and thirty thousand [black] soldiers, seamen, and laborers. These are palpable facts, about which, as facts, there can be no cavilling. We have the men; and we could not have had them without the measure." Lincoln laid heavy emphasis on the role played by the 130,000 blacks then serving in the army and navy: "And now let any Union man who complains of the measure, test himself by writing down in one line that he is for subduing the rebellion by force of arms; and in the next, that he is for taking these hundred and thirty thousand men from the Union side, and placing them where they would be but for the measure he condemns. If he can not face his case so stated, it is only because he can not face the truth."[86]

After recounting the conversation he had had with the Kentuckians, Lincoln added a postscript containing some new thoughts: "In telling this tale I attempt no compliment to my own sagacity. I claim not to have controlled events, but confess plainly that events have controlled me. Now, at the end of three years struggle the nation's condition is not what either party, or any man devised, or expected. God alone can claim it. Whither it is tending seems plain. If God now wills the removal of a great wrong, and wills also that we of the North as well as you of the South, shall pay fairly for our complicity in that wrong, impartial history will find therein new cause to attest and revere the justice and goodness of God."[87]

These concluding remarks have been misinterpreted to indicate that Lincoln was a fundamentally passive president. In fact, he was remarkably assertive in exercising control over military affairs. He took his oath of office seriously and conscientiously did what he considered his duty to preserve, protect, and defend the constitution, which meant suppressing the rebellion. In legislative matters, however, he adhered to the Whig doctrine that the president should defer to Congress. Thus, he had little to do with important economic measures passed during the war regarding tariffs, banking, taxes, homesteads, railroads, and the like. (A conspicuous exception was his promotion of a transcontinental railroad.)

In August, Lincoln emphasized the importance of the campaign when speaking to regiments that called at the White House. His iron determination to win the war shone through these remarks to the 163rd Ohio: "I wish it might be more generally and universally understood what the country is now engaged in. We have, as all will agree, a free Government, where every man has a right to be equal with every other man. In this great struggle, this form of Government and every form of human right is endangered if our enemies succeed. There is more involved in this contest than is realized by every one. There is involved in this struggle the question whether your children and my children shall enjoy the privileges we have enjoyed."[88]

A few days later, he addressed another Ohio regiment: "I almost always feel inclined, when I happen to say anything to soldiers, to impress upon them in a few brief remarks the importance of success in this contest. It is not merely for to-day, but for all time to come that we should perpetuate for our children's children this great and free government, which we have enjoyed all our lives. I beg you to remember this, not merely for my sake, but for yours. I happen temporarily to occupy this big White House. I am a living witness that any one of your children may look to come here as my father's child has. It is in order that each of you may have through this free government which we have enjoyed, an open field and a fair chance for your industry, enterprise and intelligence; that you may all have equal privileges in the race of life, with all its desirable human aspirations. It is for this the struggle should be maintained, that we may not lose our birthright—not only for one, but for two or three years. The nation is worth fighting for, to secure such an inestimable jewel."[89]

In May, Lincoln had similarly told a large audience in Philadelphia: "We accepted this war for an object, a worthy object, and the war will end when that object is attained. Under God, I hope it never will [end] until that time. . . . This war has taken three years; it was begun or accepted upon the line of restoring the national authority over the whole national domain, and for the American people, as far as my knowledge enables me to speak, I say we are going through on this line if it takes three years more."[90]

Lincoln made such public statements despite warnings that he must appease those who were calling for a compromise peace. Not only did he proclaim his willingness to continue the fight for three more years but he also resisted appeals to postpone another draft call. On July 18, he announced that five hundred thousand men would be drafted, even though he was told that such a step might cost him the election. "What is the Presidency worth to me if I have no country?" he asked.[91] "We must either have men, or the war must stop," he insisted. "I shall issue the call, and if the old ship goes down, it will be with the colors flying. So whether they come by draft, or volunteering, the nation needs soldiers. These she must have, or else she dies, and then comes anarchy, and the frightful ruin of a dismembered country, or its final surrender to the slave power, against which it now struggles, and calls every freeman to the rescue. Peace! In this struggle that which comes by the sword will be the more lasting, and worthy as a legacy to posterity."[92] He advised voters that if he was reelected, it "will mean that the rebellion is to be crushed by force of arms."[93] Democrats replied, "Tens of thousands of white men must bite the dust to allay the Negro mania of the president."[94] In mid-September, the new draft call was implemented.

As the campaign progressed, the heavy demands of office wore Lincoln down and rendered him unusually irritable. Shortly before election day, he angrily confronted a group of Tennesseans who submitted a petition complaining about the strict loyalty oath that Governor Andrew Johnson prescribed for would-be voters. The document suggested that Lincoln was selfishly and corruptly abusing his power. In response, the president asked, "May I inquire how long it took you and the New-York politicians to concoct that paper?" The delegation's spokesman asserted that it was an accurate representation of popular opinion in the Volunteer State. Lincoln scornfully remarked, "I expect to let the friends of George B. McClellan manage their side of this contest in their own way; and I will manage my side of it in my way."[95] With some justice, Democrats condemned this "undignified and rude" response as "an exhibition of party spite and petulance."[96]

William O. Stoddard, who assisted Nicolay and Hay in the White House, ascribed such presidential outbursts to stress and fatigue: "To such an extent was his absorbed devotion to business carried that the perpetual strain upon his nervous system, with the utter want of all exercise, began to tell seriously upon his health and spirits. . . . Even his temper suffered, and a petulance entirely foreign to his natural disposition was beginning to show itself as a symptom of an overtasked brain."[97] Mary Lincoln also stated that when her husband was "worn down," he "spoke crabbedly to men, harshly so."[98]

Though Lincoln grew less and less patient with the passage of time, it should be noted that, as Stoddard put it, the president "*generally* succeeds in keeping down the storm which is continually stirred up within him by the treacheries, cowardices, villainies and stupidities, which, almost daily and hourly, he is compelled to see and understand and wrestle with and overcome."[99] What is surprising is not that Lincoln lost his temper so often but rather that he lost it so seldom, considering the provocations to which he was subjected.

In October 1864, Republicans won the crucial gubernatorial elections in Indiana, Ohio, and Pennsylvania. Those victories paved the way for the party's triumph the following month. On election day in November, Lincoln reflected on the bitterness of the campaign: "It is a little singular that I who am not a vindictive man, should always have been before the people for election in canvasses marked for their bitterness: always but once: When I came Congress it was a quiet time: But always besides that the contests in which I have been prominent have been marked with great rancor."[100]

As Lincoln awaited the returns, he was joined by his good friend Assistant Secretary of the Navy Gustavus V. Fox, who openly reveled in the defeat of two congressional critics of his department. Lincoln told Fox, "You have more of that feeling of personal resentment than I. Perhaps I may have too little of it, but I never thought it paid. A man has not time to spend half his life in quarrels. If any man ceases to attack me, I never remember the past against him."[101]

When a mud-splattered member of the telegraph office staff arrived and explained that he had taken a spill in the street, Lincoln remarked, "For such an awkward fellow, I am pretty sure-footed. It used to take a pretty dextrous man to throw me. I remember, the evening of the day in 1858, that decided the contest for the Senate between Mr Douglas and myself, was something like this, dark, rainy & gloomy. I had been reading the returns, and had ascertained that we had lost the Legislature and started to go home. The path had been worn hog-back was slippery. My foot slipped from under me, knocking the other one out of the way, but I recovered myself & lit square, and I said to myself, 'It's a slip and not a fall.'"[102]

When the returns showed that Lincoln had decisively won reelection, he told a group of well-wishers, "I earnestly believe that the consequences of this day's work . . . will be to the lasting advantage, if not to the very salvation, of the country." All those "who have labored to-day in behalf of the Union organization, have wrought for the best interests of their country and the world, not only for the present, but for all future ages. I am thankful to God for this approval of the people." Yet, Lincoln was in no mood to gloat: "deeply grateful for this mark of their confidence in me, if I know my heart, my gratitude is free from any taint of personal triumph. I do not impugn the motives of any one opposed to me. It is no pleasure to me to triumph over any one; but I give thanks to the Almighty for this evidence of the people's resolution to stand by free government and the rights of humanity."[103]

Two days later, Lincoln spoke more formally about the significance of the election: "It has long been a grave question whether any government, not *too* strong for the liberties of its people, can be strong *enough* to maintain its own existence, in great emergencies. On this point the present rebellion brought our republic to a severe test; and a presidential election occurring in regular course during the rebellion added not a little to the strain. If the loyal people, *united*, were put to the utmost of their strength by the rebellion, must they not fail when *divided*, and partially paralyzed, by a political war among themselves?"[104]

But even if the danger posed by such divisions was grave, it was essential that the election be held, for "we can not have free government without elections; and if the rebellion could force us to forego, or postpone a national election, it might fairly claim to have already conquered and ruined us. The strife of the election is but human-nature practically applied to the facts of the case. What has occurred in this case, must ever recur in similar cases. Human-nature will not change. In any future great national trial, compared with the men of this, we shall have as weak, and as strong; as silly and as wise; as bad and good. Let us, therefore, study the incidents of this, as philosophy to learn wisdom from, and none of them as wrongs to be revenged."[105]

Lincoln regretted that the campaign had been so bitter, but he maintained that it "has done good too," for it "demonstrated that a people's government can sustain a national election, in the midst of a great civil war. Until now it has not been known to the world that this was a possibility. It shows also how *sound*, and how *strong* we still are. It shows that, even among candidates of the same party, he who is most devoted to the Union, and most opposed to treason, can receive most of the people's votes. It shows also, to the extent yet known, that we have more men now, than we had when the war began. Gold is good in its place; but living, brave, patriotic men, are better than gold."[106]

Lincoln urged Republicans to treat their defeated opponents mag-nanimously: "[N]ow that the election is over, may not all, having a common interest, re-unite in a common effort, to save our common country? For my own part I have striven, and shall strive to avoid placing any obstacle in the way. So long as I have been here I have not willingly planted a thorn in any man's bosom. While I am deeply sensible to the high compliment of a re-election; and duly grateful, as I trust, to Almighty God for having directed my countrymen to a right conclusion, as I think, for their own good, it adds nothing to my satisfaction that any other man may be disappointed or pained by the result. May I ask those who have not differed with me, to join with me, in this same spirit towards those who have?"[107]

Like the war, the election was widely regarded as a test of de-mocracy itself. The Massachusetts intellectual Charles Eliot Norton predicted that November 8, 1864, "will always be esteemed as one of our great historic days. Never before was a people called upon for a decision involving more vital interests not only to itself but to the progress of mankind, and never did any people show itself so worthy to be entrusted with freedom and power."[108]

Lincoln won the popular vote with 55.4 percent of the ballots cast and the electoral college vote 212 to 21. McClellan carried only Kentucky, Delaware, and New Jersey. Lincoln captured 78 percent of the soldier vote and 53 percent of the civilian vote. As a New England trooper explained, "Soldiers don't generally believe in fighting to put down treason, and voting to let it live."[109]

During the campaign, Lincoln observed, "I rely upon the religious sentiment of the country, which I am told is very largely for me."[110] He was right; evangelical Protestant churches backed him enthusiastically.

Democratic mistakes and Union victories in the field were not the only factors making Lincoln's reelection possible; voters were also expressing their approval of Lincoln personally. A correspondent of the *London Daily News* noted that rural Americans cared little about the president's manners or his taste in clothes. Instead, "his logic and his English, his jokes, his plain common sense, his shrewdness, his unbounded reliance on their honesty and straightforwardness, go right to their hearts." They "are in earnest in a way the like of which the world never saw before, silently, calmly, but deliberately in earnest; and they will fight on, in my opinion, as long as they have men, muskets, powder, and corn and wool, and would fight on, though the grass were growing in Wall Street, and there was not a gold dollar on this side of the Atlantic."[111] Lincoln's own indomitable will strengthened such resolve.

The electorate admired Lincoln's unselfishness. In early 1864, Harriet Beecher Stowe noted that of all "the many accusations which in hours of ill-luck have been thrown out upon Lincoln, it is remarkable that he has never been called self-seeking, or selfish. When we were troubled and sat in darkness, and looked doubtfully towards the presidential chair, it was never that we doubted the good-will of our pilot—only the clearness of his eyesight. But Almighty God has granted to him that clearness of vision which he gives to the true-hearted, and enabled him to set his honest foot in that promised land of freedom which is to be the patrimony of all men, black and white—and from henceforth nations shall rise up to call him blessed."[112] Wendell Phillips said in frustration, "Lincoln had won such loving trust from the people that it was impossible to argue anything against him."[113]

Other abolitionists were more enthusiastic than Phillips. Lydia Maria Child exclaimed, "Glory to God!" and rejoiced that she could finally "breathe freely now that this great danger is passed. If McClellan had been elected, the slave holders would have had it all their own way."[114] Lincoln's victory she deemed "the triumph of free schools; for it was the intelligence and reason of the people that reelected Abraham Lincoln." For all his flaws and lack of polish, the president was likable, Child acknowledged: "I have sometimes been out of patience with him; but I will say of him that I have constantly gone on liking him better and better."[115]

"Congratulate the President for me for the double victory," Grant wired Stanton. "The election having passed off quietly, no bloodshed or riot throughout the land, is a victory worth more to the country than a battle won. Rebeldom and Europe will so construe it."[116]

Rebels did indeed regard the election as a decisive blow. The chief of the Confederate bureau of war wrote that the "Yankee election was evidently a damper on the spirits of many of our people, and is said to have depressed the army a good deal. Lincoln's triumph was more complete than most of us expected."[117] A Union general in Atlanta reported that the "rebs here are much chapfallen at the disaster to their political friends in the north. They seem to consider it worse than a disaster in the field, and a death blow to their dearest hopes of success."[118] Jefferson Davis, however, refused to surrender. Rather than acknowledge the obvious fact that the Confederacy could not win its independence, he resolved to fight on, needlessly prolonging a lost war for another five bloody months.

CHAPTER ELEVEN

ENDGAME

At Lincoln's urging, the 1864 Republican convention called for
a constitutional amendment abolishing slavery throughout
the nation, not just in the Confederate states. Lincoln had limited
the scope of the Emancipation Proclamation to areas in rebellion
because he believed that the Constitution did not authorize him to
liberate slaves elsewhere. But if emancipation was established by a
constitutional amendment, then no such limitation would apply.

In June, the House of Representatives had failed to approve the
Thirteenth Amendment by the necessary two-thirds majority. Six
months later, Lincoln told Congress that the election results constituted a mandate in favor of the amendment and urged its adoption.
Abandoning his usual reticence in dealing with legislative measures,
Lincoln threw himself into the effort to pass the amendment. With
the help of Secretary of State William Henry Seward, whose agents
offered reluctant congressmen various inducements (among them
patronage favors and money), Lincoln managed to obtain the necessary two-thirds vote in favor of the amendment, which passed on
January 31, 1865. Lincoln was gratified that Illinois was the first state
to ratify it; by year's end, enough other states had followed suit to
make it part of the Constitution. Then slavery was officially dead
everywhere in the nation.

The amendment almost failed to pass when rumors reached the
House that Confederate peace negotiators were en route to Washington. Lincoln managed to reassure skittish lawmakers with a

misleading statement: "So far as I know, there are no peace commissioners in the city, or likely to be in it."[1] Lincoln was well aware that Confederate commissioners were to meet with Seward at Hampton Roads, Virginia, to discuss peace terms. That meeting had been arranged after would-be peace brokers from the North had visited Richmond and spoken with Jefferson Davis. On February 2, Lincoln himself traveled to Hampton Roads to participate in the negotiations, which went nowhere. The Confederates were unwilling to accept Lincoln's three preconditions for peace: cessation of hostilities, restoration of the Union, and the abolition of slavery.

Lincoln's support of the Thirteenth Amendment pleased the Radicals, as did his selection of a replacement for Chief Justice of the U.S. Supreme Court Roger B. Taney, who died in October 1864. Several candidates vied for the position, including three members of Lincoln's initial cabinet—Salmon P. Chase, Montgomery Blair, and Edward Bates—as well as distinguished lawyers like William M. Evarts. (In November, Bates had resigned as attorney general, to be replaced by James Speed of Kentucky, brother of Lincoln's closest friend, Joshua Speed.)

Lincoln hesitated to name Chase, partly because of the former treasury secretary's insatiable desire to become president. Chase, he said, "is a man of unbounded ambition, and has been working all his life to become President; that he can never be; and I fear that if I make him Chief Justice, he will simply become more restless and uneasy, and neglect the place in his strife and intrigue to make himself President. He has got the Presidential maggot in his head and it will wriggle there as long as it is warm. If I were sure that he would go upon the bench and give up his aspirations to do anything but make himself a great judge, I would send in his name at once."[2] When champions of Evarts's candidacy urged Lincoln to "crush out" Chase, the president said, "Chase is a very able man" who was, to be sure, "a little insane" on the presidency and who "has not always behaved very well lately." But that was not enough to disqualify him for a seat on the Supreme Court: "I'm not in favor of crushing anybody out! If there is anything a man can do and do it well, I say let him do it. Give him a chance."[3]

Despite these reservations, Lincoln nominated Chase to be chief justice, explaining that the selection was made "in deference to what he supposed to be public sentiment," for the Ohioan "occupies the largest place in the public mind in connection with the office."[4]

"Probably no other man than Lincoln," John G. Nicolay remarked, "would have had, in this age of the world, the degree of magnanimity to thus forgive and exalt a rival who had so deeply and so unjustifiably intrigued against him. It is however only another most marked illustration of the greatness of the President, in this age of little men."[5] Nicolay was right, for Lincoln declared that if his personal feelings were to be considered, he would rather "swallow his buckhorn chair" or "eat flat irons" than name Chase to the high court.[6]

In the wake of his reelection, Lincoln came under pressure to appoint other men to office, for many Republicans looked upon the president's second term as the occasion for "a new deal."[7] But Lincoln was in no mood to oblige them. "I have made up my mind to make very few changes in the offices in my gift for my second term," he said. "I think now that I will not remove a single man except for delinquency. To remove a man is very easy, but when I go to fill his place, there are twenty applicants, and of these I must make nineteen enemies."[8] A congressman speculated that Lincoln "will go along without many changes because of his aversion to do anything that he thinks would be unpleasant to anyone."[9]

To escape importunate would-be civil servants, Lincoln often visited the theater, which he regarded as a kind of sanctuary. In March 1865, a colonel who joined him at an opera performance recalled that the president said he attended the event "for the rest. I am being hounded to death by office-seekers, who pursue me early and late, and it is simply to get two or three hours' relief that I am here."[10]

In the weeks after the election, Lincoln was so busy fending off the office seekers and preparing his annual message to Congress that he had no time to respond to an appeal to offer condolences to a Boston woman who had purportedly lost five sons in the war. So the president had John Hay write such a document, which became famous as the "letter to the widow Bixby." Unaware that Hay composed it, many admirers of the beautiful letter have mistakenly ranked it with the

Gettysburg Address and the second inaugural as one of Lincoln's greatest prose masterpieces.[11]

The second inaugural richly deserves that reputation, however. By the time Lincoln delivered it on March 4, 1865, the war was clearly about to end. In the four preceding months, William T. Sherman had marched across Georgia from Atlanta to Savannah and had penetrated into the Carolinas. In Tennessee, George H. Thomas had destroyed John Bell Hood's army in pitched battles at Franklin and Nashville. In Virginia, Philip Sheridan had crushed Jubal Early in the Shenandoah Valley, and Ulysses S. Grant's siege of Petersburg was wearing down Robert E. Lee's army so badly that it would be forced to abandon Richmond within a month. In North Carolina, the last hole in the Union blockade had been plugged at the Battle of Wilmington. In Alabama, Mobile was on the verge of surrender.

As the war wound down, Lincoln sought to pave the way for a magnanimous peace by defusing Northern vindictiveness, which was strong in many circles. A prominent Unitarian minister argued that in dealing with Confederacy, the North "shall be compelled to *exterminate* her 300,000 slaveholders."[12] A former mayor of Chicago insisted that the "extermination of the rebel whites" was essential.[13] Some abolitionists favored a policy of "conquest & extermination, not the killing of every man woman & child, but the destruction & decimation of the ruling classes & an entire social reorganization."[14] Lincoln's new vice president, Andrew Johnson of Tennessee, declared that "treason must be made odious" and "traitors must be impoverished, their social power broken." Rich Confederates must be arrested, tried, convicted, and hanged, Johnson said: "We have put down these traitors in arms; let us put them down in law, in public judgment, and in the morals of the world."[15]

In the closing paragraph of his unusually brief second inaugural address, Lincoln counseled against such a punitive spirit: "With malice toward none; with charity for all; with firmness in the right, as God gives us to see the right, let us strive on to finish the work we are in; to bind up the nation's wounds; to care for him who shall have borne the battle, and for his widow, and his orphan—to do all which may achieve and cherish a just, and a lasting peace, among ourselves, and with all nations."[16]

In a remarkable meditation on God's will, Lincoln also sought to undermine Northern self-righteousness. The president had long tried to understand why the Almighty had allowed the war to begin and why He had allowed it to continue so long. In a private memorandum written earlier in the war, he wrestled with that question: "The will of God prevails. In great contests each party claims to act in accordance with the will of God. Both *may* be, and one *must* be, wrong. God cannot be *for* and *against* the same thing at the same time. In the present civil war it is quite possible that God's purpose is something different from the purpose of either party—and yet the human instrumentalities, working just as they do, are of the best adaptation to effect His purpose. I am almost ready to say that this is probably true—that God wills this contest, and wills that it shall not end yet. By his mere quiet power, on the minds of the now contestants, He could have either *saved or destroyed* the Union without a human contest. Yet the contest began. And, having begun He could give the final victory to either side any day. Yet the contest proceeds."[17]

Addressing that question in his second inaugural, Lincoln suggested that the war was God's punishment on both North and South for the sin of slavery. He began by stating, "The Almighty has His own purposes." He then quoted Jesus from the Gospel according to Saint Matthew (8:17): "Woe unto the world because of offences! for it must needs be that offences come; but woe to that man by whom the offence cometh!" Lincoln then applied those words to the Civil War: "If we shall suppose that American Slavery is one of those offences which, in the providence of God, must needs come, but which, having continued through His appointed time, He now wills to remove, and that He gives to both North and South, this terrible war, as the woe due to those by whom the offence came, shall we discern therein any departure from those divine attributes which the believers in a Living God always ascribe to Him? Fondly do we hope—fervently do we pray—that this mighty scourge of war may speedily pass away. Yet, if God wills that it continue, until all the wealth piled by the bond-man's two hundred and fifty years of unrequited toil shall be sunk, and until every drop of blood drawn with the lash, shall be paid by another drawn with the sword, as was said three thousand years ago, so still it must be said 'the judgments of the Lord, are true and righteous altogether.'"[18]

Lincoln's desire for a generous peace did not sit well with the Radicals who opposed the Ten Percent Plan that he had announced in December 1863. Led by Massachusetts Senator Charles Sumner, they managed to thwart the president by refusing to recognize the legitimacy of Southern state governments created under the Ten Percent Plan. Lincoln had hoped that the regime established in Louisiana would serve as a model for the other ten Confederate states. Over 10 per cent of the voters there had taken an oath of future loyalty, had adopted a constitution abolishing slavery, and elected a governor, a state legislature, and U.S. senators and congressmen. Radicals objected that the constitution did not enfranchise blacks. Lincoln, too, was disappointed by that omission. In early 1864, he had written to the newly elected governor of the Bayou State suggesting that some black men be allowed to vote.[19]

While Lincoln was willing to endorse black suffrage in private, he was unwilling to do so publicly until April 11, 1865, when he delivered what was to be his last speech. Two days earlier, Lee had surrendered to Grant, and the war was over, for all practical purposes. No longer did Lincoln feel the need to induce the Confederates to lay down their arms by offering them exceptionally easy peace terms. Now he felt free to align himself more closely with the Radicals on Reconstruction. He would still favor generous amnesty and pardon for most Confederates, but he would assert publicly for the first time his support for black voting rights. In his April 11 speech (which he did not know would be his final one), he said apropos of the Louisiana state constitution, "It is also unsatisfactory to some that the elective franchise is not given to the colored man. I would myself prefer that it were now conferred on the very intelligent, and on those who serve our cause as soldiers."[20]

Some Radicals were disappointed by the limited scope of Lincoln's proposal. Frederick Douglass, who heard the president's speech, at first thought that it "seemed to mean but little," but later he concluded that it actually "meant a great deal. It was just like Abraham Lincoln. He never shocked prejudices unnecessarily. Having learned statesmanship while splitting rails, he always used the thin edge of the wedge first—and the fact that he used it at all meant that he would if need be, use the thick as well as the thin."[21] This endorsement of limited black suffrage helped convince Douglass that Lincoln should be considered "emphatically the black man's President: the first to show any respect for their rights as men . . . the first American President who . . . rose above the prejudice of his times, and country."[22]

One member of Lincoln's audience on April 11 did not underestimate its importance: John Wilkes Booth. Upon hearing the words about black voting rights, the young actor declared, "That means nigger citizenship. Now, by God, I'll put him through."[23] He added, "That is the last speech he will ever make."[24] And so it was, for three days later Booth shot Lincoln to death.

Lincoln was not murdered because he had issued the Emancipation Proclamation or because he endorsed the Thirteenth Amendment. He was killed because he endorsed the enfranchisement of blacks, and therefore Lincoln should be considered a martyr to black citizenship rights, as much as Martin Luther King Jr., or Medgar Evers, or Viola Liuzzo, or Mickey Schwerner, or James Reeb, or James Cheney, or Andrew Goodman, or any of the others who were killed in the 1960s as they championed the civil rights movement.

Lincoln's successor, vice president Andrew Johnson, was a Tennessee racist who had none of Lincoln's statesmanlike qualities. Frederick Douglass had abundant reason to declare, in late 1865, "Whosoever else have cause to mourn the loss of Abraham Lincoln, to the colored people of the country his death is an unspeakable calamity."[25]

Lincoln was more than the "black man's president" or "the Great Emancipator"; he was also "the savior of the Union." But he was also more than that; by leading a successful war to preserve "government of the people, by the people, and for the people," he was "the Vindicator of Democracy." He succeeded because he somehow managed to be strong-willed without being willful, moral without being moralistic, and righteous without being self-righteous; because he inspired confidence and affection; because he had a preternatural understanding of public opinion; because his sense of political timing was exquisite; because he had developed an extraordinarily high level of psychological maturity and balance; because he managed to infuse his indomitable will into the Northern public; because he masterfully kept the Republican party (and by extension the North itself) unified; and because he was supremely eloquent in articulating the aims of the war. Without those qualities, he would have failed, the North would have lost the war, slavery would have long persisted, and the cause of democracy in the world would have received a severe setback.

ACKNOWLEDGMENTS

As I worked on this volume and various other Lincoln books over the past quarter century, I have been the beneficiary of support from so many generous patrons, hospitable friends and family, helpful librarians, and fellow scholars that I hesitate to mention them by name lest I inadvertently omit some. I cannot refrain, however, from thanking my better-half-to-be, the lovely and long-suffering Lois Erickson McDonald, who over the past two decades has been an unflagging source of support and love, without which I could not have written this book and the others.

As both an undergraduate and a graduate student, I had the good fortune to work under an eminent Lincolnian, the late David Herbert Donald. If he had been a medievalist, I probably would have specialized in the history of the Middle Ages.

At Southern Illinois University Press, which has published several of my collections of Lincoln-related primary source materials, I am especially grateful to Sylvia Frank Rodrigue and her colleagues.

NOTES

Introduction

1. Hanchett, *Out of the Wilderness: The Life of Abraham Lincoln* (Urbana: University of Illinois Press, 1994), 60.
2. Beauregard, "The First Battle of Bull Run," Robert Underwood Johnson and Clarence Clough Buel, eds., *Battles and Leaders of the Civil War* (4 vols.: New York: Century, 1887–88), 1:222.
3. Rhodes, *Lectures on the American Civil War* (New York: Macmillan, 1913), 99.
4. Randall, "Abraham Lincoln," *Dictionary of American Biography*, 11:258.
5. Potter, "Jefferson Davis and the Political Factors in Confederate Defeat," in *Why the North Won the Civil War*, ed. David Donald (Baton Rouge: Louisiana State University Press, 1960), 111.
6. McPherson, "American Victory, American Defeat," in *Why the Confederacy Lost*, ed. Gabor S. Boritt (New York: Oxford University Press, 1992), 37.
7. Leonard Swett to William H. Herndon, Chicago, 17 January 1866, in *Herndon's Informants: Letters, Interviews, and Statements about Abraham Lincoln*, ed. Douglas L. Wilson and Rodney O. Davis (Urbana: University of Illinois Press, 1998), 165. Hereafter cited as HI.
8. Lincoln to James M. Cutts, Washington, 26 October 1863, Roy P. Basler et al., eds., *The Collected Works of Abraham Lincoln* (8 vols. plus index; New Brunswick, N. J.: Rutgers University Press, 1953–55), 6:538. Hereafter cited as CWL.
9. CWL, 8:101.
10. On Lincoln's cruel streak, see Michael Burlingame, *The Inner World of Abraham Lincoln* (Urbana: University of Illinois, 1994), 149–55.
11. CWL, 3:511, 4:67.
12. See Daniel J. Levinson et al., *The Seasons of a Man's Life* (New York: Knopf, 1978).
13. CWL, 2:382–83.
14. John G. Nicolay, "Abraham Lincoln," speech of 14 April 1894, Nicolay MSS, Library of Congress.
15. *Our Constitution* (Urbana), 4 July 1857.
16. Herndon to Jesse W. Weik, Springfield, 7, 10 January 1886, Herndon-Weik MSS, LC.
17. Notes for a law lecture, Roy P. Basler, ed., *Collected Works of Abraham Lincoln, First Supplement* (Westport, Conn.: Greenwood Press, 1974), 18.
18. Herndon to Jesse W. Weik, [Springfield], 15 December 1886, Herndon-Weik MSS, LC.

19. Herndon, "Facts Illustrative of Mr. Lincoln's Patriotism and Statesman-ship," *Abraham Lincoln Quarterly* 3 (1944–45): 188–89.

20. Speed to Herndon, Louisville, 7 February 1866, HI, 197.

21. Lincoln to John D. Johnston, Springfield, 12 January 1851, CWL, 2:97.

22. Emerson, journal entry for 31 January 1862, Louis P. Masur, ed., *The Real War Will Never Get in the Books: Selections from Writers during the Civil War* (New York: Oxford University Press, 1993), 127.

23. Herndon, "Lincoln Individually," Herndon-Weik MSS, LC.

24. Speed, *Reminiscences of Abraham Lincoln and Notes of a Visit to California: Two Lectures* (Louisville: J. P. Morton, 1884), 34.

25. Speed to Herndon, Louisville, 6 December 1866, HI, 499.

26. Nathan M. Knapp to O. M. Hatch, Winchester, Illinois, 12 May 1859, Hatch MSS, Abraham Lincoln Presidential Library and Museum, Springfield, Illinois. Hereafter cited as ALPLM.

27. John H. Littlefield, "Recollections of One Who Studied Law with Lincoln," William Hayes Ward, ed., *Abraham Lincoln, Tributes from His Associates: Reminiscences of Soldiers, Statesmen, and Citizens* (New York: Thomas Y. Crowell, 1895), 204–5.

28. Francis Grierson, *The Valley of Shadows: Recollections of the Lincoln Country, 1858–1863* (Boston: Houghton Mifflin, 1909), 200.

29. A document in Gillespie's MSS, quoted in Josephine G. Pricket, "Joseph Gillespie," *Transactions of the Illinois State Historical Society for the Year 1912* (publication no. 17 of the Illinois State Historical Library), 108.

30. Henry C. Whitney, "Abraham Lincoln: A Study from Life," *Arena* 19 (1898): 466.

31. Swisshelm in Allen Thorndike Rice, ed., *Reminiscences of Abraham Lincoln by Distinguished Men of His Time* (New York: North American, 1886), 413.

32. E. J. Edwards, quoting the conductor, Gilbert Finch, then retired and residing in Connecticut, New York *Times*, 24 January 1909.

33. Noah Brooks, "Personal Recollections of Abraham Lincoln," *Harper's New Monthly Magazine*, July 1865, in Michael Burlingame, ed., *Lincoln Observed: Civil War Dispatches of Noah Brooks* (Baltimore: Johns Hopkins University Press, 1998), 211.

34. Undated statement by a Dr. Parker, in John G. Nicolay's hand, Nicolay-Hay MSS, ALPLM.

35. Michael Burlingame and John R. Turner Ettlinger, eds., *Inside Lincoln's White House: The Complete Civil War Diary of John Hay* (Carbondale: Southern Illinois University Press, 1997), 69 (entry for 31 July 1863). Hereafter cited as JHD.

36. James Russell Lowell, "Abraham Lincoln," *The Writings of James Russell Lowell* (12 vols.; Cambridge: Riverside Press, 1890–92), 5:208.

37. Horace White, *Abraham Lincoln in 1854* (Springfield: Illinois State Historical Society, 1908), 21.

38. Diary of Joseph T. Mills, 19 August 1864, CWL, 7:507.

1. The Election of 1860 and Southern Secession

1. J. K. Moorhead, interview with John G. Nicolay, Washington, 12 and 13 May 1880, *An Oral History of Abraham Lincoln: John G. Nicolay's Interviews and Essays*, ed. Michael Burlingame (Carbondale: Southern Illinois University Press, 1996), 41.

2. David Kilgore to Richard W. Thompson, Indianapolis, Indiana, 5 September 1860, Richard W. Thompson Collection, Lincoln Financial Collection, Allen County Public Library, Fort Wayne, Indiana.

3. James H. Reed to John J. Crittenden, Greenwich, Connecticut, 17 January 1861, Crittenden Papers, Library of Congress. Library of Congress hereafter cited as LC.

4. David A. Wells to Andrew Johnson, Troy, New York, 29 December 1860, Johnson Papers, LC.

5. George Henry Calvert to John Pendleton Kennedy, Newport, Rhode Island, 5 January 1861, John Pendleton Kennedy Papers, Enoch Pratt Free Library, Baltimore.

6. Horace Greeley to Salmon P. Chase, New York, 28 September 1858, Chase Papers, Historical Society of Pennsylvania, Philadelphia.

7. *New York World*, 23 October 1860.

8. *The Collected Works of Abraham Lincoln*, ed. Roy P. Basler et al., 8 vols. plus index (New Brunswick, NJ: Rutgers University Press, 1953–55), 2:501. Hereafter cited as *CWL*.

9. James Henry Thornwell of the Columbia, South Carolina, Presbyterian Theological Seminary, "The State of the Country," pamphlet (New Orleans: True Witness and Sentinel Office, 1861), in *Southern Pamphlets on Secession, November 1860–April 1861*, ed. Jon L. Wakelyn (Chapel Hill: University of North Carolina Press, 1996), 162.

10. Kenneth Rayner to Caleb Cushing, Raleigh, North Carolina, 9 December 1860, Caleb Cushing Papers, LC.

11. See Charles B. Dew, *Apostles of Disunion: Southern Secession Commissioners and the Causes of the Civil War* (Charlottesville: University Press of Virginia, 2001).

12. Alexander H. Stephens, speech delivered in Savannah, Georgia, 21 March 1861, in Henry Cleveland, *Alexander H. Stephens, in Public and Private with Letters and Speeches, before, during, and since the War* (Philadelphia: National, 1866), 721.

13. *Atlanta (GA) Gate-City Guardian*, 23 February 1861.

14. *Richmond (VA) Daily Dispatch*, 20 November 1861.

15. *Congressional Globe*, 36th Congress, 2nd session, 212 (31 December 1860).

16. *New Orleans (LA) Bee*, 10 December 1860.

17. Clarence Phillips Denman, *The Secession Movement in Alabama* (Montgomery: Alabama State Department of Archives and History, 1933), 8.

18. John Bell to Alexander Robinson Boteler, 30 July 1860, quoted in Joseph Howard Parks, *John Bell of Tennessee* (Baton Rouge: Louisiana State University Press, 1950), 365.

19. Peter V. Daniel to Martin Van Buren, Richmond, Virginia, 1 November 1847, Martin Van Buren Papers, LC.

20. *Congressional Globe*, 31st Congress, 1st session, appendix, 149 (13 February 1850).

21. *CWL*, 4:439. Kentucky Senator John J. Crittenden's proposal long commanded respect among historians, although modern scholars are much less enthusiastic about it. Harold M. Hyman, "The Narrow Escape from a 'Compromise of 1860': Secession and the Constitution," in *Freedom and Reform: Essays in Honor of Henry Steele Commager*, ed. Harold M. Hyman and Leonard W. Levy (New York: Harper & Row, 1967), 158–59.

22. William Kellogg to Lincoln, Washington, 6 December 1860, Lincoln Papers, LC; Lincoln to Kellogg, Springfield, 11 December 1860, *CWL*, 4:150.

23. Lincoln to E. B. Washburne, Springfield, Illinois, 13 December 1860, *CWL*, 4:151.

24. Charles Francis Adams diary, 22 December 1860, Adams Family Papers, Massachusetts Historical Society, Boston.

25. Henry Wilson to William S. Robinson, Washington, D.C., 16 December 1860, in William S. Robinson, *"Warrington" Pen-Portraits: A Collection of Personal and Political Reminiscences* (Boston: Lee and Shepard, 1877), 93.

26. That charge is made most explicitly in Duff Green, *Facts and Suggestions: Biographical, Historical, Financial, and Political* (New York: Westcott, 1866), 225–26. See also David M. Potter, *Lincoln and His Party in the Secession Crisis* (New Haven: Yale University Press, 1942).

27. *CWL*, 4:141–42.

28. Lincoln to Henry J. Raymond, 28 November 1860, *CWL*, 4:145–46.

29. *CWL*, 4:150.

30. *Springfield, Illinois State Journal*, 17 December 1860.

31. Frank Blair to Montgomery Blair, St. Louis, Missouri, n.d. [15 December 1860], Blair Family Papers, Princeton University.

32. Joshua Speed to Gideon Welles, Louisville, 8 August 1872, Abraham Lincoln Collection, Beinecke Library, Yale University.

33. John W. Bunn to Isaac N. Phillips, Springfield, Illinois, 8 November 1910, in *Abraham Lincoln by Some Men Who Knew Him*, (originally ed. Isaac N. Phillips) ed. Paul M. Angle (1910; Chicago: Americana House, 1950), 114–15.

34. J. K. Moorhead, interview with John G. Nicolay, Washington, 12 and 13 May 1880, in Burlingame, *Oral History of Lincoln*, 41.

35. William B. Campbell to A. C. Beard, 15 March 1861, quoted in Daniel W. Crofts, *Reluctant Confederates: Upper South Unionists in the Secession Crisis* (Chapel Hill: University of North Carolina Press, 1989), xvi.

36. William M. Clark to Lewis Thompson, 10 January 1861, in Crofts, *Reluctant Confederates*, xvi.

2. From Election to Inauguration

1. John G. Nicolay, memorandum, 22 December 1860, in *With Lincoln in the White House: Letters, Memoranda, and Other Writings of John G. Nicolay, 1860–1865*, ed. Michael Burlingame (Carbondale: Southern Illinois University Press, 2000), 21.

2. J[ames] H. v[an] A[len] to Horace Greeley, St. Louis, Missouri, 21 December 1860, Horace Greeley Papers, New York Public Library.

3. *Chicago Tribune*, 15 May 1861, in Silvana R. Siddali, "'The Sport of Folly and the Prize of Treason': Confederate Property Seizures and the Northern Home Front in the Secession Crisis," *Civil War History* 47 (2001): 332.

4. *Memoirs of John Adams Dix*, ed. Morgan Dix, 2 vols. (New York: Harper, 1883), 1:345.

5. *The Collected Works of Abraham Lincoln*, ed. Roy P. Basler et al., 8 vols. plus index (New Brunswick, NJ: Rutgers University Press, 1953–55), 4:195–96. Hereafter cited as *CWL*.

6. [John Hay], Philadelphia correspondence, 21 February, *New York World*, 22 February 1861, in *Lincoln's Journalist: John Hay's Anonymous Writings for the Press, 1860–1864*, ed. Michael Burlingame (Carbondale: Southern Illinois University Press, 1998), 38.

7. George Alfred Townsend, undated clipping, *San Francisco Chronicle*, Lincoln Financial Collection, Allen County Public Library, Fort Wayne, Indiana.

8. *CWL*, 4:266.

9. *CWL*, 4:246–47.

10. John A. Bingham, "Abraham Lincoln," speech delivered at Cadiz, Ohio, 15 April 1886, *Chicago Current*, 24 April 1886, 282.

11. *CWL*, 4:271.

12. *CWL*, 4:262–70.

13. Ibid.

14. Ibid.
15. (Entry for 6 March 1861), Benjamin Brown French, *Witness to the Young Republic: A Yankee's Journal, 1828–1870*, ed. Donald B. Cole and John J. McDonough (Hanover, NH: University Press of New England, 1989), 348.
16. *Charleston (SC) Mercury*, 5 March 1861.

3. The Fort Sumter Crisis

1. *The Collected Works of Abraham Lincoln*, ed. Roy P. Basler et al., 8 vols. plus index (New Brunswick, NJ: Rutgers University Press, 1953–55), 4:424. Hereafter cited as *CWL*.
2. Martin Crawford, ed., *William Howard Russell's Civil War: Private Diary and Letters, 1861–1862* (Athens: University of Georgia Press, 1992), 26.
3. John G. Nicolay and John Hay, *Abraham Lincoln: A History*, 10 vols. (New York: Century, 1890), 3:371.
4. William B. Plato to Lyman Trumbull, Geneva, Kane County, Illinois, 29 March 1861, Trumbull Papers, Library of Congress.
5. *New York Times*, 24 December 1860.
6. *CWL*, 4:424.
7. William Henry Seward to his wife, Washington, 5 June 1861, in Frederick W. Seward, *William H. Seward: An Autobiography from 1801 to 1834, with a Memoir of His Life, and Selections from His Letters*, 3 vols. (New York: Derby and Miller, 1891), 2:590.
8. *CWL*, 8:332.
9. (Entry for 9 February 1861), in *The Diary of Orville Hickman Browning*, ed. Theodore Calvin Pease and James G. Randall, 2 vols. (Springfield: Trustees of the Illinois State Historical Library, 1925–33), 1:453.

4. The War Begins

1. Lincoln to Erastus Corning and others, Washington, 12 June 1863, *The Collected Works of Abraham Lincoln*, ed. Roy P. Basler et al., 8 vols. plus index (New Brunswick, NJ: Rutgers University Press, 1953–55), 6:263. Hereafter cited as *CWL*.
2. *CWL*, 2:124.
3. *CWL*, 5:537.
4. Washington correspondence, 12 April, *New York World*, 13 April 1861; Washington correspondence, 12 April, *Cincinnati Gazette*, n.d, reprinted in the *Springfield, Illinois State Register*, 16 April 1861.
5. Benjamin Brown French to his son Frank, Washington, 14 April 1861, French Family Papers, Library of Congress. Library of Congress hereafter cited as LC.

6. John G. Nicolay and John Hay, *Abraham Lincoln: A History*, 10 vols. (New York: Century, 1890), 4:7.

7. *CWL*, 4:331–32.

8. William C. Rives to Robert C. Winthrop, Castle Hill, VA, 19 April 1861, Winthrop Family Papers, Massachusetts Historical Society, Boston.

9. George W. Brown, *Baltimore and the Nineteenth of April 1861: A Study of the War* (Baltimore: Murray, 1887), 74.

10. S. Teackle Wallis to James Alfred Pearce, Baltimore, MD, 18 July 1861, in Bernard C. Steiner, "James Alfred Pearce," *Maryland Historical Magazine* 19 (1924): 26.

11. Lincoln, message to Congress, 4 July 1861, first draft in Lincoln's hand, Lincoln Papers, LC.

12. Edward Kirkwood to Gideon Welles, Brattleboro, Vermont, 16 April 1861, Gideon Welles Papers, LC.

13. James R. Doolittle to Lyman Trumbull, Racine, Wisconsin, 24 April 1861, Lyman Trumbull Papers, LC.

14. Lyman Trumbull to his wife Julia, Washington, 2 July 1861, Trumbull Family Papers, Abraham Lincoln Presidential Library and Museum, Springfield, Illinois.

15. *CWL*, 5:241–42.

16. *Washington, D.C., States and Union*, 15 April 1861.

17. Diary of Clifford Arrick, 20 April 1861, Frontier Guard Records, LC.

18. Nicolay and Hay, *Abraham Lincoln*, 4:152.

19. Lincoln, quoted in speech by B. F. Watson, *Boston Evening Journal*, 16 April 1911.

20. *CWL*, 5:24.

21. *Baltimore Sun*, 23 April 1861.

22. Washington correspondence 29 April 1861, *Cincinnati Gazette*, 3 May 1861.

23. George T. M. Davis to Prosper M. Wetmore, New York, 1 May 1861, in John Austin Stevens, *The Union Defence Committee of the City of New York: Minutes, Reports, and Correspondence* (New York: Union Defence Committee, 1885), 154.

24. (Entry for 24 April 1861), *Inside Lincoln's White House: The Complete Civil War Diary of John Hay*, ed. Michael Burlingame and John R. Turner Ettlinger (Carbondale: Southern Illinois University Press, 1997), 11.

25. Washington correspondence, 28 April, *New York Times*, 1 May 1861.

26. *CWL*, 4:372.

27. Douglas Wilson's version of the second printed draft with Lincoln's emendations, Papers, Abraham Lincoln Papers, Library of Congress.

28. Wilbourn E. Benton, ed., *1787: Drafting the U.S. Constitution*, 2 vols. (College Station: Texas A & M University Press, 1986), 1:976, 991.

29. George Lunt to Caleb Cushing, Newburyport, Massachusetts, 11 July 1861, Cushing Papers, LC.

30. Lincoln to Orville H. Browning, Washington, 22 September 1861, *CWL*, 4:532.

31. John W. Forney, Washington correspondence, 11 September 1861, *Philadelphia Press*, 12 September 1861.

32. John W. Forney, reminiscences, *New York Evening Post*, 30 November 1865.

33. Charles Gibson to "My dear Sir," Washington, 13 May 1861, Gibson Papers, Missouri Historical Society, St. Louis.

34. Edward Everett, journal, 23 August 1861, Edward Everett Papers, Massachusetts Historical Society, Boston.

35. William H. Seward to Charles F. Adams, 21 May 21 1861, draft, Abraham Lincoln Papers, Library of Congress.

36. Carl Schurz, *The Reminiscences of Carl Schurz*, 3 vols. (New York: McClure, 1907–8), 2:242.

37. William B. Wilson, *A Few Acts and Actors in the Tragedy of the Civil War in the United States* (Philadelphia: privately printed, 1892), 111; Lincoln to Oliver P. Morton, Washington, 29 September 1861, *CWL*, 4:541.

38. Lincoln to E. D. Morgan, Washington, 20 May 1861, *CWL*, 4:375.

39. Washington correspondence by "Au Revoir," 20 July 1861, *St. Louis Missouri Democrat*, 25 July 1861.

40. *CWL*, 4:421–41.

41. Ibid.

42. Ibid.

43. Ibid.

44. Ibid.

45. Ibid.

46. Edward Cary, *George William Curtis* (Boston: Houghton Mifflin, 1894), 147.

47. *Springfield, Illinois State Journal*, 9 July 1861; *Douglass' Monthly*, 4, August 1861, 497.

48. James A. Hamilton, *Reminiscences of James A. Hamilton; or, Men and Events, at Home and Abroad, during Three Quarters of a Century* (New York: Scribner, 1869), 477.

49. *New York Tribune*, 26 June 1861.

50. Washington correspondence by Special, 31 May 1861, *Cincinnati Commercial*, 1 June 1861.

51. U.S. Congress, *Report of the Joint Committee on the Conduct of the War*, 3 vols. (Washington, DC, 1863), 2:38.

52. George P. Goff to John G. Nicolay, Washington, 9 February 1889, Nicolay Papers, LC.

53. Washington correspondence, 5 August 1861, *National Antislavery Standard* (New York), 10 August 1861.

54. *CWL*, 4:457–58.

55. (Entry for 2 April 1862), in *The Diary of Orville Hickman Browning*, ed. Theodore Calvin Pease and James G. Randall, 2 vols. (Springfield: Trustees of the Illinois State Historical Library, 1925–33), 1:537–38.

5. Stalemate

1. Benjamin Brown French to his son Frank, Washington, 8 December 1861, French Family Papers, LC. Library of Congress hereafter cited as LC.

2. Stephen W. Sears, ed., *The Civil War Papers of George B. McClellan: Selected Correspondence, 1860–1865* (New York: Ticknor and Fields, 1989), 70, 71.

3. Ibid., 71–75.

4. Ibid., 81.

5. Ibid., 107.

6. (Entry for [November 1861]), *Inside Lincoln's White House: The Complete Civil War Diary of John Hay*, ed. Michael Burlingame and John R. Turner Ettlinger (Carbondale: Southern Illinois University Press, 1997), 30. Hereafter cited as JHD.

7. Michael Burlingame, *The Inner World of Abraham Lincoln* (Urbana: University of Illinois Press, 1994), 182.

8. (Entry for 13 November 1861), JHD, 32.

9. F. A. Mitchell to John Hay, East Orange, New Jersey, 3 January 1889, Nicolay-Hay Papers, Abraham Lincoln Presidential Library and Museum, Springfield, Illinois.

10. Sears, *Civil War Papers of George B. McClellan*, 106–7.

11. Stephen W. Sears, *George B. McClellan: The Young Napoleon* (New York: Ticknor & Fields, 1988), 116–17.

12. James Russell Lowell to Jane Norton, Elmwood, 28 September 1861, *Letters of James Russell Lowell*, ed. Charles Eliot Norton, 2 vols. (New York: Harper, 1894), 1:314.

13. Benjamin F. Wade to Zachariah Chandler, Jefferson, Ohio, 23 September 1861, Chandler Papers, LC.

14. *New York Herald*, n.d., reprinted in *Boston Liberator*, 27 September 1861.

15. Lincoln to Orville H. Browning, Washington, 22 September 1861, in *The Collected Works of Abraham Lincoln*, ed. Roy P. Basler et al., 8 vols. plus index (New Brunswick, NJ: Rutgers University Press, 1953–55), 4:531–32. Hereafter cited as *CWL*.

16. *CWL*, 4:531–32.

17. Richard Yates to Gustave Koerner, Springfield, 25 October 1861, *Memoirs of Gustave Koerner, 1809–1896*, ed. Thomas J. McCormack, 2 vols. (Cedar Rapids, IA: Torch, 1909), 2:188.
18. (Entry for 28 November 1863), JHD, 123.
19. Richard Smith to Chase, Cincinnati, 7 November 1861, Chase Papers, LC.
20. Charles E. Pike to James S. Pike, Oshkosh, Wisconsin, 2 October (continuation of a letter begun on 15 September) 1861, Pike Papers, University of Maine, Orono.
21. Hans L. Trefousse, *The Radical Republicans: Lincoln's Vanguard for Racial Justice* (New York: Knopf, 1969), 184.
22. Zachariah Chandler to his wife, Washington, 27 October 1861, Chandler Papers, LC.
23. *CWL*, 5:91–92.
24. *CWL*, 5:95.
25. M. C. Meigs, "The Relations of President Lincoln and Secretary Stanton to the Military Commanders in the Civil War," *American Historical Review* 26 (1921): 292.
26. Horace Porter, *Campaigning with Grant* (New York: Century, 1897), 407–8.
27. John Eaton, *Grant, Lincoln and the Freedmen: Reminiscences of the Civil War* (New York: Longmans, Green, 1907), 178.

6. War in Earnest

1. *Oregonian* (Portland, OR), 20 May 1862.
2. Washington correspondence, 19 January 1862, *Philadelphia Inquirer*, 20 January 1862.
3. Edwards Pierrepont to Lincoln, New York, 19 January 1862, Abraham Lincoln Papers, Library of Congress.
4. *The Collected Works of Abraham Lincoln*, ed. Roy P. Basler et al., 8 vols. plus index (New Brunswick, NJ: Rutgers University Press, 1953–55), 5:98–99. Hereafter cited as *CWL*.
5. Wendell Phillips, speech in Boston, 17 April 1862, in *Boston Liberator*, 25 April 1862; Noyes W. Miner to John Y. Scammon et al., Belvidere, Illinois, 1 August 1871, *Quincy (IL) Whig*, 16 March 1872, reprinted in the *New York Times*, 23 March 1872.
6. "Miriam" (Mrs. John A. Kasson), Washington correspondence, 20 February 1862, *Des Moines, Iowa State Register*, 1 March 1862.
7. Henry A. Wise to A. H. Foote, Washington, 23 January 1862, in *CWL*, 5:108.
8. Henry A. Wise to A. H. Foote, Washington, 31 January 1862, William P. Palmer Collection, Western Reserve Historical Society, Cleveland, Ohio.

9. (Entry for March 1862), in *Inside Lincoln's White House: The Complete Civil War Diary of John Hay*, ed. Michael Burlingame and John R. Turner Ettlinger (Carbondale: Southern Illinois University Press, 1997), 35. Hereafter cited as JHD.

10. Joseph E. Johnston to Robert E. Lee, Lee's Farm, Virginia, 22 April 1862, in *The War of the Rebellion: A Compilation of the Official Records of the Union and Confederate Armies*, 128 vols. (Washington, DC: GPO, 1880–1901), series 1, vol. 11, part 3, 456.

11. Howard K. Beale, ed., *Diary of Gideon Welles, Secretary of the Navy under Lincoln and Johnson*, 3 vols. (New York: Norton, 1960), 1:124.

12. Stephen W. Sears, *George B. McClellan: The Young Napoleon* (New York: Ticknor & Fields, 1988), 180.

13. George B. McClellan to Edwin M. Stanton, Savage Station, Virginia, 28 June 1862, in *The Civil War Papers of George B. McClellan: Selected Correspondence, 1860–1865*, ed. Stephen W. Sears (New York: Ticknor and Fields, 1989), 323.

14. Washington correspondence, 6 August, *Cincinnati Gazette*, 11 August 1862.

15. George W. Bell to John Sherman, Lawrence, Kansas, 23 July 1862, John Sherman Papers, Library of Congress.

16. Van [D. W. Bartlett], Washington correspondence, 22 July 1862, *Springfield, Massachusetts, Republican*, 24 July 1862; Washington correspondence, 21 July 1862, *Cincinnati Gazette*, 22 July 1862; Washington correspondence, 22 July 1862, *New York Evening Post*, 23 July 1862.

17. Lincoln to Cuthbert Bullitt, Washington, DC, 28 July 1862, *CWL*, 5:344–46.

18. Sears, *Civil War Papers of George B. McClellan*, 402.

19. (Entry for [1 September 1862]), JHD, 37.

20. Joseph T. Glatthaar, *Partners in Command: The Relationships between Leaders in the Civil War* (New York: Free Press, 1994), 237–42.

21. (Entries for 7, 8 September 1862), Beale, *Diary of Gideon Welles*, 1:113, 116.

22. (Entry for [1 September 1862]), JHD, 37–38.

23. Beale, *Diary of Gideon Welles*, 1:105.

7. Dealing with Slavery

1. *The Collected Works of Abraham Lincoln*, ed. Roy P. Basler et al., 8 vols. plus index (New Brunswick, NJ: Rutgers University Press, 1953–55), 5:336–37. Hereafter cited as *CWL*.

2. Montgomery Blair, "The Republican Party as It Was and Is," *North American Review* 131 (1880): 426.

3. *Douglass' Monthly*, January 1863, 642.

4. Washington correspondence, 29 December 1862, *New York Tribune*, 30 December 1862.

5. *CWL*, 5:537.

6. Moncure Conway, *Autobiography, Memories and Experiences of Moncure Daniel Conway*, 2 vols. (London: Cassell, 1904), 1:379.

7. Edward Everett Hale, *Memories of a Hundred Years*, 2 vols. (New York: Macmillan, 1903), 2:193; F. B. Carpenter, *Six Months at the White House with Abraham Lincoln: The Story of a Picture* (New York: Hurd and Houghton, 1867), 90; Ida M. Tarbell, *The Life of Abraham Lincoln*, 2 vols. (New York: Lincoln Memorial Association, 1900), 2:97–98.

8. Albert G. Brown Jr., *Sketch of the Official Life of John A. Andrew as Governor of Massachusetts* (New York: Hurd and Houghton, 1868), 74–75; Henry Greenleaf Pearson, *The Life of John A. Andrew, Governor of Massachusetts, 1861–1865*, 2 vols. (Boston: Houghton Mifflin, 1904), 2:51.

9. *Douglass' Monthly*, October 1862, 721.

10. *Harper's Weekly*, 4 October 1862.

11. Montgomery Blair to Lincoln, Washington, 23 July 1862, Chase Papers, Library of Congress.

12. *Chicago Times*, 24 September 1862; *Boston Post*, n.d., reprinted in the *Springfield (MA) Republican*, 24 September 1862.

13. *New York Evening Express*, 23 September 1862.

14. *New York Tribune*, 16 October 1862.

15. Allan Nevins, *The War for the Union*, 4 vols. (New York: Scribner, 1959–71), 2:319.

16. *Columbus (OH) Crisis*, 5 March 1862; *Cincinnati Enquirer*, 4 August 1862.

17. Hezekiah S. Bundy to Salmon P. Chase, Reid's Mill, Ohio, 18 October 1862, Salmon P. Chase Papers, Library of Congress.

18. Reginald Charles McGrane, *William Allen: A Study in Western Democracy* (Columbus: Ohio State Archaeological and Historical Society, 1925), 157–58.

8. Winter of Discontent

1. Lincoln to George B. McClellan, Washington, 25 October 1862, in *The Collected Works of Abraham Lincoln*, Roy P. Basler et al., 8 vols. plus index (New Brunswick, NJ: Rutgers University Press, 1953–55), 5:474. Hereafter cited as *CWL*.

2. O. M. Hatch, interviewed by Nicolay, Springfield, June 1875, in *An Oral History of Abraham Lincoln: John G. Nicolay's Interviews and Essays*, ed. Michael Burlingame (Carbondale: Southern Illinois University Press, 1996), 16.

3. *CWL*, 5:460–61.

4. Adams S. Hill to Sydney Howard Gay, Washington, 13 October 1862, in Louis M. Starr, *Bohemian Brigade: Civil War Newsmen in Action* (New York: Knopf, 1954), 152.

5. Francis P. Blair Sr. to Francis P. Blair Jr., 7 November 1862, and Francis P. Blair Sr. to Montgomery Blair, 2 March 1863, Blair Family Papers, Library of Congress. Library of Congress hereafter cited as LC.

6. Stephen W. Sears, *George B. McClellan: The Young Napoleon* (New York: Ticknor & Fields, 1988), xii.

7. Horace Porter, *Campaigning with Grant* (New York: Century, 1897), 415.

8. Horace White to Lincoln, Chicago, 22 October 1862, Abraham Lincoln Papers, LC.

9. John Niven, ed., *The Salmon P. Chase Papers*, 5 vols. (Kent, OH: Kent State University Press, 1993–98), 3:294–95.

10. *The War of the Rebellion: A Compilation of the Official Records of the Union and Confederate Armies*, 128 vols. (Washington, DC: GPO, 1880–1901), series 1, vol. 16, part 2, 626–27. Hereafter cited as *OR*.

11. Ibid., 643; John F. Marszalek, *Commander of All Lincoln's Armies: A Life of General Henry W. Halleck* (Cambridge, MA: Belknap Press of Harvard University Press, 2004), 153.

12. Henry L. Dawes to his wife, Washington, 10 December 1862, Henry L. Dawes Papers, LC.

13. *Baltimore American*, 26 March 1864, in J. T. Dorris, "President Lincoln's Clemency," *Lincoln Herald* 55 (1953): 6; William Henry Wadsworth to S. L. M. Barlow, Washington, 16 December 1862, S. L. M. Barlow Papers.

14. Howard K. Beale, ed., *Diary of Gideon Welles, Secretary of the Navy under Lincoln and Johnson*, 3 vols. (New York: Norton, 1960), 1:201–2.

15. Burlingame, *Oral History of Lincoln*, 87.

16. (Entry for 30 October 1863), in *Inside Lincoln's White House: The Complete Civil War Diary of John Hay*, ed. Michael Burlingame and John R. Turner Ettlinger (Carbondale: Southern Illinois University Press, 1997), 104.

17. Madeleine Vinton Dahlgren, *Memoir of John A. Dahlgren, Rear-Admiral, United States Navy* (Boston: Osgood, 1882), 383–84.

18. "Occasional" (John W. Forney), column, *Washington Sunday Chronicle*, 3 December 1865.

19. William P. Fessenden to his son William, Washington, 21 December 1862, Fessenden Papers, Bowdoin College, Brunswick, Maine; Fessenden to his father, Washington, 20 December 1862, Fessenden Papers; Fessenden to James S. Pike, Portland, Maine, 5 April 1863, Pike Papers, LC.

20. Beale, *Diary of Gideon Welles*, 2:280.

21. Lincoln to William S. Rosecrans, Washington, 5 January 1863, 31 August 1863, *CWL*, 6:39, 424–25.

22. William O. Stoddard, *Inside the White House in War Times: Memoirs and Reports of Lincoln's Secretary*, ed. Michael Burlingame (Lincoln: University of Nebraska Press, 2000), 101.

23. Lincoln to Joseph Hooker, Washington, 26 January 1863, *CWL*, 6:78–79.

24. Gideon Welles, *Lincoln and Seward* (New York: Sheldon, 1874), 200.

25. Noah Brooks, *Abraham Lincoln and the Downfall of American Slavery* (New York: Putnam's, 1896), 358.

26. John Sherman to William T. Sherman, Mansfield, Ohio, 7 May 1863, William T. Sherman Papers, LC.

27. "Lincoln as the Loneliest Man," clipping, *Drayter [?] Gleaner*, 2 November 1937, Lincoln Financial Collection, Allen County Public Library, Fort Wayne, Indiana.

9. The Tide Turns

1. D. W. Bartlett, Washington correspondence, 6 June 1863, *New York Independent*, 11 June 1863.

2. *Chicago Republican*, n.d., reprinted in the *New York Evening Post*, 14 June 1865.

3. Washington correspondence, 25 May 1863, *Philadelphia Inquirer*, n.d., reprinted in the *Chicago Tribune*, 29 May 1863.

4. *The Collected Works of Abraham Lincoln*, ed. Roy P. Basler et al., 8 vols. plus index (New Brunswick, NJ: Rutgers University Press, 1953–55), 6:326. Hereafter cited as *CWL*.

5. *CWL*, 6:409.

6. *CWL*, 6:364.

7. George S. Boutwell in *Reminiscences of Abraham Lincoln by Distinguished Men of His Time*, ed. Allen Thorndike Rice (New York: North American, 1886), 128.

8. Allan Nevins, *The War for the Union*, 4 vols. (New York: Scribner, 1959–71), 3:95.

9. John Hay to John Nicolay, Washington, 7 August 1863, in *At Lincoln's Side: John Hay's Civil War Correspondence and Selected Writings*, ed. Michael Burlingame (Carbondale: Southern Illinois University Press, 2000), 49.

10. George C. Gorham, *Life and Public Services of Edwin M. Stanton*, 2 vols. (Boston: Houghton Mifflin, 1899), 2:99.

11. James B. Fry in Rice, *Reminiscences of Abraham Lincoln*, 402.

12. (Entry for 14 July 1863), *Inside Lincoln's White House: The Complete Civil War Diary of John Hay*, ed. Michael Burlingame and John R. Turner Ettlinger (Carbondale: Southern Illinois University Press, 1997), 62. Hereafter cited as JHD.

13. Albert B. Chandler, "Lincoln and the Telegrapher," *American Heritage* 12 (1961): 32–34.

14. (Entry for 14 July 1863), JHD, 62.

15. Robert Todd Lincoln interviewed by John Nicolay, 5 January 1885, in *An Oral History of Abraham Lincoln: John G. Nicolay's Interviews and Essays*, ed. Michael Burlingame (Carbondale: Southern Illinois University Press, 1996), 88–89.

16. David Davis to Julius Rockwell, Bloomington, Illinois, 19 August 1863, David Davis Papers, Library of Congress. Library of Congress hereafter cited LC.

17. Lincoln to George Gordon Meade, Washington, 14 July 1863, *CWL*, 6:327–28.

18. William A. Croffut, *An American Procession, 1855–1914: A Personal Chronicle of Famous Men* (Boston: Little, Brown, 1931), 102.

19. George William Curtis to Charles Eliot Norton, North Shore, New York, 12 July 1863, George William Curtis Papers, Harvard University.

20. George D. Morgan to George G. Fogg, Irvington, 24 November 1863, George E. Fogg Papers, New Hampshire Historical Society, Concord.

21. John Hay to John Nicolay, Washington, 7 August 1863 and 11 September 1863, in Burlingame, *At Lincoln's Side*, 49, 54.

22. Jennifer L. Weber, *Copperheads: The Rise and Fall of Lincoln's Opponents in the North* (New York: Oxford University Press, 2006).

23. Don E. Fehrenbacher and Virginia Fehrenbacher, eds., *Recollected Words of Abraham Lincoln* (Stanford: Stanford University Press, 1996), 288.

24. *The War of the Rebellion: A Compilation of the Official Records of the Union and Confederate Armies*, 128 vols. (Washington, DC: GPO, 1880–1901), series 1, vol. 23, part 2, 237–38.

25. *New York Tribune*, 3 October 1863.

26. *CWL*, 6:406–10.

27. Ibid.

28. Israel Washburn Jr. to Lincoln, Orono, Maine, 15 September 1863, Abraham Lincoln Papers, LC.

29. Charles Eliot Norton to George William Curtis, Cambridge, Massachusetts, 3 September 1863, in *Letters of Charles Eliot Norton*, ed. Sara Norton and M. A. De Wolfe Howe, 2 vols. (Boston: Houghton Mifflin, 1913), 1:263.

30. (Entry for 24 October 1863), JHD, 99.

31. Lincoln to Robert A. Maxwell, Washington, 23 September 1863, *CWL*, 6:475.

32. *CWL*, 7:36–53.

33. Lincoln to Michael Hahn, Washington, 13 March 1864, *CWL*, 7:243.

34. Petition dated 10 March 1864, *Boston Liberator*, 1 April 1864.

35. Frederick Douglass to George Luther Stearns, Philadelphia, Pennsylvania, 12 August 1863, copy, Records of the Free Military School for Command of Colored Regiments, Historical Society of Pennsylvania, Philadelphia; Douglass, speech, 4 December 1863, in *The Frederick Douglass Papers, Series One: Speeches, Debates, and Interviews*, ed. John W. Blassingame et al., 5 vols. (New Haven: Yale University Press, 1979–92), 3:606–8.

36. Douglass in Rice, *Reminiscences of Abraham Lincoln*, 322; John Eaton, *Grant, Lincoln, and the Freedmen: Reminiscences of the Civil War* (New York: Longmans, Green, 1907), 175–76.

37. Lincoln to Edwin M. Stanton, Washington, 5 February 1864, *CWL*, 7:169.

38. John P. Hale to his wife, 29 May 1864, in Richard H. Sewell, *John P. Hale and the Politics of Abolition* (Cambridge: Harvard University Press, 1965), 210.

39. Worthington G. Snethen to Wendell Phillips, Baltimore, Maryland, 25 August 1864, Wendell Phillips Papers, Harvard University.

40. Washington correspondence, 28 February 1864, *Chicago Tribune*, 3 March 1864.

10. Reelection

1. John D. Defrees to Josiah G. Holland, Washington, 8 August 1865, J. G. Holland Papers, New York Public Library, in Allen C. Guelzo, "Holland's Informants: The Construction of Josiah Holland's 'Life of Abraham Lincoln,'" *Journal of the Abraham Lincoln Association* 23 (2002): 45; Thurlow Weed to John Bigelow, in John Bigelow, *Retrospections of an Active Life*, 5 vols. (New York: Baker and Taylor, 1909–13), 2:110; (entry for 29 October 1863), *Inside Lincoln's White House: The Complete Civil War Diary of John Hay*, ed. Michael Burlingame and John R. Turner Ettlinger (Carbondale: Southern Illinois University Press, 1997), 103. *Inside Lincoln's White House* hereafter cited as JHD.

2. John B. Alley in *Reminiscences of Abraham Lincoln by Distinguished Men of His Time*, ed. Allen Thorndike Rice (New York: North American, 1886), 581–82.

3. (Entries for 29 and 18 October 1863 and for [July–August 1863]), JHD, 103, 93, 78.

4. Lincoln to Salmon P. Chase, Washington, 29 February 1864, in *The Collected Works of Abraham Lincoln*, ed. Roy P. Basler et al., 8 vols. plus index (New Brunswick, NJ: Rutgers University Press, 1953–55), 7:212–13. Hereafter cited as *CWL*.

5. John P. Usher, *President Lincoln's Cabinet* (Omaha, NE, 1925), 14.

6. Washington correspondence, 26 February 1864, *Columbus Ohio State Journal*, 1 March 1864.

7. David Davis to Julius Rockwell, Washington, 25 February 1864, David Davis Papers, Library of Congress. Library of Congress hereafter cited as LC.

8. Noah H. Swayne to Samuel J. Tilden, Washington, 19 February 1864, Samuel J. Tilden Papers, New York Public Library.

9. (Entry for 30 June 1864), JHD, 212.

10. John Brough quoted in William Henry Smith, private memoranda, in JHD, 354.

11. William D. Kelley to the editor of the *New York Tribune*, Philadelphia, 23 September 1885, in William D. Kelley, *Lincoln and Stanton* (New York: Putnam's, 1885), 86; (entry for 1 July 1864), JHD, 216.

12. *At Lincoln's Side: John Hay's Civil War Correspondence and Selected Writings*, ed. Michael Burlingame (Carbondale: Southern Illinois University Press, 2000), 110.

13. *Diary and Letters of Rutherford Birchard Hayes*, ed. Charles R. Williams, 5 vols. (Columbus: Ohio State Archaeological and Historical Society, 1922–26), 3:242, 243.

14. B. Rush Plumly to N. P. Banks, New Orleans, 20 October 1864, Nathaniel Prentiss Banks Papers, LC.

15. (Entry for 30 June 1864), JHD, 212–15.

16. (Entry for 22 May 1864), JHD, 197–98.

17. F. B. Carpenter, *Six Months at the White House with Abraham Lincoln: The Story of a Picture* (New York: Hurd and Houghton, 1867), 220–21.

18. Oscar Sherwin, *Prophet of Liberty: The Life and Times of Wendell Phillips* (New York: Bookman, 1958), 493; Irving H. Bartlett, *Wendell Phillips: Brahmin Radical* (Boston: Beacon, 1961), 269.

19. *Boston Liberator*, 18 March 1864.

20. William Lloyd Garrison to Francis Newman, 15 July 1864, in *The Letters of William Lloyd Garrison*, ed. Walter M. Merrill, 6 vols. (Cambridge, MA: Belknap Press of Harvard University Press, 1971–81), 5:180.

21. Auguste Laugel, (diary entry for 24 September 1864), in *The United States during the Civil War*, ed. Allan Nevins (Bloomington: Indiana University Press, 1961), 302.

22. *Boston Liberator*, n.d., reprinted in the *National Anti-Slavery Standard* (New York), 8 October 1864.

23. Owen Lovejoy to William Lloyd Garrison, 22 February 1864, *Boston Liberator*, n.d., reprinted in the *Columbus Ohio State Journal*, 8 April 1864.

24. Owen Lovejoy, *His Brother's Blood: Speeches and Writings, 1838–64*, ed. William F. Moore and Jane Ann Moore (Urbana: University of Illinois Press, 2004), 380, 389.

25. Carpenter, *Six Months at the White House*, 47–48.

26. Horace Greeley to Lincoln, New York, 7 July 1864, Abraham Lincoln Papers, LC.

27. Shelby M. Cullom, *Fifty Years of Public Service: Personal Recollections of Shelby M. Cullom, Senior United States Senator from Illinois* (Chicago: McClurg, 1911), 101.

28. Lincoln to "whom it may concern," Washington, [1]8 July 1864, *CWL*, 8:63.

29. *Cincinnati Enquirer*, 25 July 1864.

30. *Detroit Free Press*, n.d., reprinted in the *New York World*, 29 July 1864.

31. *Reading (PA) Gazette and Democrat*, 30 July 1864, and *Johnstown (PA) Democrat*, 17 August 1864, in Arnold M. Shankman, *The Pennsylvania Antiwar Movement, 1861–1865* (Rutherford, NJ: Fairleigh Dickinson University Press, 1980), 180.

32. (Entry for 19 August 1864), *The Diary of George Templeton Strong, 1835–1875*, ed. Allan Nevins and Milton Halsey Thomas, 4 vols. (New York: Macmillan, 1952), 3:474.

33. Joseph E. McDonald, interview in the *Pittsburgh (PA) Commercial*, n.d, reprinted in the *New York Times*, 28 December 1882.

34. Interview with Alexander W. Randall and Joseph T. Mills, 19 August 1864, *CWL*, 7:506–7.

35. Charles D. Robinson to Lincoln, Green Bay, Wisconsin, 7 August 1864, Abraham Lincoln Papers, LC.

36. Lincoln to Charles D. Robinson, Washington, 17 August 1864, draft, *CWL*, 7:500.

37. Douglass, speech at Rochester, New York, 18 April 1865, *Washington Daily Morning Chronicle*, 27 April 1865.

38. Frederick Douglass to Theodore Tilton, Rochester, New York, 15 November 1864, in Philip S. Foner, *The Life and Writings of Frederick Douglass*, 5 vols. (New York: International, 1950), 3:422–24.

39. On the controversy surrounding this interpretation, see James McPherson, "Who Freed the Slaves?" in McPherson, *Drawn with the Sword: Reflections on the American Civil War* (New York: Oxford University Press, 1996), 192–215.

40. Memorandum, 23 August 1864, *CWL*, 7:514.

41. (Entry for 11 November 1864), JHD, 248.

42. John Murray Forbes to John A. Andrew, New York, 2 September 1864, John A. Andrew Papers, Massachusetts Historical Society, Boston; Forbes to Charles Eliot Norton, Naushon, Massachusetts, 25 August 1864, Charles Eliot Norton Papers, Harvard University.

43. Wendell Phillips to Elizabeth Cady Stanton, n.p., 27 September 1864, in Alma Lutz, *Susan B. Anthony: Rebel, Crusader, Humanitarian* (Boston: Beacon, 1959), 106.

44. Wendell Phillips, speech, October 20, 1864, Boston, in Oscar Sherwin, *Prophet of Liberty: A Biography of Wendell Phillips* (New York: New York University Press, 1943), 505.

45. Maria Weston Chapman to Lizzie Chapman Laugel, Weymouth, Massachusetts, 23 February 1864, Weston Sisters Papers, Boston Public Library.

46. *Boston Liberator*, 28 October 1864.

47. Wendell Garrison to Ellie Garrison, 12 July 1864, in Harriet Hyman Alonso, *Growing Up Abolitionist: The Story of the Garrison Children* (Amherst: University of Massachusetts Press, 2002), 218–19.

48. Parker Pillsbury to Wendell Phillips, Concord, New Hampshire, 27 August 1864, Wendell Phillips Papers, Harvard University.

49. William D. Kelley to J. Miller McKim, Washington, 1 May 1864, copy, William Lloyd Garrison Papers, Boston Public Library.

50. J. W. Rathbone to Manton Marble, Albany, New York, 4 November 1864, Manton Marble Papers, LC.

51. Nevins and Thomas, *Diary of George Templeton Strong*, 3:480–81.

52. John Nicolay to Theodore Tilton, Washington, 6 September 1864, Miscellaneous Manuscripts, New-York Historical Society, New York City.

53. John Nicolay to Therena Bates, Washington, 11 September 1864, *With Lincoln in the White House: Letters, Memoranda, and Other Writings of John G. Nicolay, 1860–1865*, ed. Michael Burlingame (Carbondale: Southern Illinois University Press, 2000), 158.

54. John Frémont to George L. Stearns et al., Nahant, Massachusetts, 17 September 1864, *Boston Daily Advertiser*, 23 September 1864.

55. Frederick Douglass to Theodore Tilton, Rochester, New York, 15 October 1864, in Foner, *Life and Writings of Frederick Douglass*, 3:424; *Boston Liberator*, 23 February 1864.

56. Cyrus [Bearenderfer?] to Daniel Musser, 20 February 1864, in Shankman, *Pennsylvania Antiwar Movement, 1861–1865*, 196.

57. Interview with Alexander W. Randall and Joseph T. Mills, 19 August 1864, *CWL*, 7:508.

58. John McMahon to Lincoln, Harmbrook, Pennsylvania, 5 August 1864, John G. Nicolay Papers, LC.

59. John Nicolay to John McMahon, Washington, 6 August 1864, *CWL*, 7:483.

60. *Columbus (OH) Crisis*, 3 August 1864, in David Lindsey, *"Sunset" Cox, Irrepressible Democrat* (Detroit: Wayne State University Press, 1959), 84; *Cleveland Plain Dealer*, n.d., in Elizabeth F. Yager, "The Presidential Campaign of 1864 in Ohio," *Ohio Archaeological and Historical Quarterly* 34 (1925): 571–72.

61. Kenneth Silverman, *Lightning Man: The Accursed Life of Samuel F. B. Morse* (New York: Knopf, 2003), 410–11.

62. Yager, "Presidential Campaign of 1864 in Ohio," 572–73; *Cincinnati Enquirer*, 23 and 24 September 1864.

63. James J. Farran to Alexander Long, Cincinnati, 26 June 1864, Alexander Long Papers, Cincinnati Historical Society.

64. *Columbus, Ohio, Crisis*, 27 January 1864, in Reed W. Smith, *Samuel Medary & the Crisis: Testing the Limits of Press Freedom* (Columbus: Ohio State University Press, 1995), 130.

65. *La Crosse (WI) Daily Democrat*, 25 August 1864.

66. Hans L. Trefousse, *First among Equals: Abraham Lincoln's Reputation during His Administration* (New York: Fordham University Press, 2005), 112.

67. Carl Sandburg's notes of an interview with Joseph Fifer, [1923], Carl Sandburg–Oliver Barrett Collection, Newberry Library, Chicago.

68. Orville H. Browning to [Edgar] Cowan, Quincy, Illinois, 6 September 1864, photostatic copy, J. G. Randall Papers, LC.

69. Elizabeth Keckley, *Behind the Scenes* (New York: Carleton, 1868), 146.

70. James H. Linsley to Miss Conant, Bermuda Hundred, Virginia, 16 June 1864, TS, Schoff Civil War Collection, William L. Clements Library, University of Michigan.

71. A. H[omer] B[yington] to [Sydney Howard] Gay, Washington, 23 March [1864]; Sam Wilkeson to Sydney Howard Gay, [Washington, ca. 23 March 1864], Sydney Howard Gay Papers, Columbia University.

72. Keckley, *Behind the Scenes*, 149–50.

73. McPherson, *Political History of the United States*, 364.

74. Edwin M. Stanton to Benjamin F. Butler, Washington, 17 November 1863, in *The War of the Rebellion: A Compilation of the Official Records of the Union and Confederate Armies*, 128 vols. (Washington, DC: GPO, 1880–1901), series 2, 6:528. Hereafter this compilation cited as *OR*.

75. Michael Burlingame, *The Inner World of Abraham Lincoln* (Urbana: University of Illinois Press, 1994), 194–95.

76. Washington correspondence, 16 October, *New York Tribune*, 17 October 1864.

77. W. A. Croffut, ed., *Fifty Years in Camp and Field: Diary of Major-General Ethan Allen Hitchcock, U.S.A.* (New York: Putnam's, 1909), 458.

78. (Entry for 17 June 1864), JHD, 207–8.

79. Don E. Fehrenbacher and Virginia Fehrenbacher, eds., *Recollected Words of Abraham Lincoln* (Stanford: Stanford University Press, 1996), 529.

80. (Entry for 28 October 1863), JHD, 101.

81. (Entry for 10 December 1863), JHD, 125.

82. Lincoln to Charles D. Drake and others, Washington, 5 October 1863, *CWL*, 6:500.

83. Leonard Swett, speech, 22 October 1880, *Chicago Times*, 23 October 1880.

84. E. W. Andrews in Rice, *Reminiscences of Abraham Lincoln*, 518.

85. Leonard Swett to William H. Herndon, 1887, in *Herndon's Informants: Letters, Interviews, and Statements about Abraham Lincoln*, ed. Douglas L. Wilson and Rodney O. Davis (Urbana: University of Illinois Press, 1998), 165n.

86. Lincoln to Albert Hodges et al., Washington, 4 April 1864, *CWL*, 7:281–82.

87. Ibid.

88. *CWL*, 7:504–5.

89. Speech to the 166th Ohio Regiment, 22 August 1864, *CWL*, 7:512.

90. Speech, 19 May 1864, *CWL*, 7:395.

91. John G. Nicolay and John Hay, *Abraham Lincoln: A History*, 10 vols. (New York: Century, 1890), 9:364.

92. Washington correspondence by R. S. B., 20 August 1864, *Philadelphia Inquirer*, 22 August 1864.

93. Ida M. Tarbell, *The Life of Abraham Lincoln*, 2 vols. (New York: Lincoln Memorial Association, 1900), 2:195.

94. *Columbus, Ohio, Crisis*, 3 August 1864, in Smith, *Samuel Medary & the Crisis*, 91.

95. John Lellyett to the editors of the *Washington National Intelligencer*, 15 October 1864, in McPherson, *Political History of the United States*, 439.

96. *New York Daily News*, 18 and 25 October 1864.

97. William O. Stoddard, "White House Sketches, No. 11," *New York Citizen*, 27 October 1866, in Stoddard, *Inside the White House in War Times*, ed. Burlingame, 190.

98. Mary Lincoln, interview with William H. Herndon, September 1866, *HI*, 361.

99. Stoddard, *Inside the White House in War Times*, 29–30.

100. (Entry for 8 November 1864), JHD, 243.

101. Ibid., 245.

102. Ibid., 244–45.

103. *CWL*, 8:96.

104. *CWL*, 8:100–101.

105. Ibid.

106. Ibid.

107. Ibid.

108. Charles Eliot Norton to George Perkins Marsh, Cambridge, Massachusetts, 29 December 1864, George Perkins Marsh Papers, University of Vermont, Burlington.

109. Emil Rosenblatt and Ruth Rosenblatt, eds., *Anti-Rebel: The Civil War Letters of Wilbur Fisk* (Croton-on-Hudson, NY: Rosenblatt, 1983), 276.

110. Joseph P. Thompson in *Our Martyred President: Voices from the Pulpit of New York and Brooklyn* (New York: Tibbal and Whiting, 1865), 191.

111. Dispatch dated 10 September, *London Daily News*, 27 September 1864, in Allan Nevins, *The War for the Union*, 4 vols. (New York: Scribner, 1959–71), 4:103, 141–42.

112. Stowe in *Littell's Living Age*, 6 February 1864.

113. Wendell Phillips to Elizabeth Cady Stanton, 23 April 1865, Ida Husted Harper Collection, Huntington Library, San Marino, California, quoted in Don E. Fehrenbacher, *Lincoln in Text and Context: Collected Essays* (Stanford: Stanford University Press, 1987), 203.

114. Lydia Maria Child to John Fraser, Wayland, Massachusetts, 10 November 1864, *The Collected Correspondence of Lydia Maria Child, 1817–1880*, ed. Patricia G. Holland, Milton Meltzer, and Francine Krasno (Millwood, NY: Kraus Microform, 1980).

115. Lydia Maria Child to Eliza Scudder, Wayland, Massachusetts, 14 November 1864, Samuel J. May Antislavery Collection, Cornell University.

116. Ulysses S. Grant to Edwin M. Stanton, City Point, Virginia, 10 November 1864, *OR*, series 1, vol. 42, part 3, 581.

117. (Entry for 20 November 1864), Edward Younger, ed., *Inside the Confederate Government: The Diary of Robert Garlick Hill Kean, Head of the Bureau of War* (New York: Oxford University Press, 1957), 177.

118. J. W. Geary to his wife, Atlanta, 24 November 1864, in *A Politician Goes to War: The Civil War Letters of John White Geary*, ed. William Alan Blair (University Park: Pennsylvania State University Press, 1995), 211.

11. Endgame

1. Lincoln to James M. Ashley, Washington, 31 January 1865, in *The Collected Works of Abraham Lincoln*, ed. Roy P. Basler et al., 8 vols. plus index (New Brunswick, NJ: Rutgers University Press, 1953–55), 8:248; James M. Ashley to William H. Herndon, Toledo, Ohio, 23 November 1866, *Herndon's Informants: Letters, Interviews, and Statements about Abraham Lincoln*, ed. Douglas L. Wilson and Rodney O. Davis (Urbana: University of Illinois Press, 1998), 413–14. The first work is hereafter cited as *CWL*.

2. Henry Wilson interviewed by John G. Nicolay, Washington, 1 April 1874, in *An Oral History of Abraham Lincoln: John G. Nicolay's Interviews and Essays*, ed. Michael Burlingame (Carbondale: Southern Illinois University Press, 1996), 85.

3. Memo by Ebenezer Rockwood Hoar enclosed in Hoar to James Ford Rhodes, Concord, Massachusetts, 9 February 1894, James Ford Rhodes Papers, Massachusetts Historical Society, Boston.

4. Jacob W. Schuckers to William Maxwell Evarts, 11 June 1875, in Brainerd Dyer, *The Public Career of William M. Evarts* (Berkeley: University of California Press, 1933), 157n; George S. Boutwell, *Reminiscences of Sixty Years in Public Affairs*, 2 vols. (New York: McClure, Phillips, 1902), 2:29.

5. John G. Nicolay to Therena Bates, Washington, 8 December 1864, *With Lincoln in the White House: Letters, Memoranda, and Other Writings of John G. Nicolay, 1860–1865*, ed. Michael Burlingame (Carbondale: Southern Illinois University Press, 2000), 166.

6. (Entry for 15 December 1864), in *Diary of Gideon Welles, Secretary of the Navy under Lincoln and Johnson*, ed. Howard K. Beale, 3 vols. (New York: Norton, 1960), 2:196; Virginia Woodbury Fox diary, 10 December 1864, Levi Woodbury Papers, Library of Congress. Library of Congress hereafter cited as LC.

7. Washington correspondence by Noah Brooks, 10 January, *Sacramento, California, Daily Union*, 22 February 1865, in *Lincoln Observed: Civil War Dispatches of Noah Brooks*, ed. Michael Burlingame (Baltimore: Johns Hopkins University Press, 1998), 157.

8. F. B. Carpenter, *Six Months at the White House with Abraham Lincoln: The Story of a Picture* (New York: Hurd and Houghton, 1867), 276.

9. Samuel Hooper to Salmon P. Chase, Washington, 10 March 1865, Salmon P. Chase Papers, Historical Society of Pennsylvania, Philadelphia.

10. James Grant Wilson, "Recollections of Lincoln," *Putnam's Magazine* 5, February 1909, 529.

11. Michael Burlingame, "The Authorship of the Bixby Letter," in *At Lincoln's Side: John Hay's Civil War Correspondence and Selected Writings*, ed. Burlingame (Carbondale: Southern Illinois University Press, 2000), 169–84.

12. Henry W. Bellows to Cyrus Augustus Bartol, Walpole, New Hampshire, 18 August 1862, Henry W. Bellows Papers, Massachusetts Historical Society, Boston.

13. Mahlon D. Ogden to James R. Doolittle, Chicago, 6 August 1862, James R. Doolittle Papers, State Historical Society of Wisconsin, Madison.

14. Edward Lillie Pierce to N. P. Banks, Boston, 15 September 1862, N. P. Banks Papers, LC.

15. *Washington Daily Morning Chronicle*, 4 April 1865.

16. *CWL*, 8:332–33.

17. *CWL*, 5:403–4.

18. *CWL*, 8:332–33.

19. Lincoln to Michael Hahn, Washington, 13 March 1864, *CWL*, 7:243.

20. *CWL*, 8:400.

21. Frederick Douglass, manuscript of a speech, [ca. December 1865], Frederick Douglass Papers, LC.

22. Frederick Douglass, manuscript of a speech given in New York, 1 June 1865, ibid.

23. Louis J. Weichmann, *A True History of the Assassination of Abraham Lincoln and of the Conspiracy of 1865*, ed. Floyd E. Risvold (New York: Knopf, 1975), 148.

24. "Impeachment of the President," *House Report No. 7*, 40th Congress, 1st session (1867), 674.

25. Frederick Douglass, manuscript of a speech, [ca. December 1865], Frederick Douglass Papers, LC.

INDEX

abolition and abolitionists, 58, 60, 67, 98–99, 125
Adams, Charles Francis, 15, 42
Albany (NY) Atlas and Argus (newspaper), 105
Albert (Prince), 57
Allen, William, 71
amalgamation, 104
Anaconda Plan, proposed, 48
Anderson, Robert, 28, 40–41
Andersonville prison, Georgia, 108
Andrew, John A., 69
Antietam, battle of (Maryland), 66–67
Army of the Cumberland, 86
Army of Northern Virginia, 80–81
Army of the Ohio, 83–84
Army of the Potomac (Division of the Potomac): at Battle of Fredericksburg, 74, 77; Hooker and, 77–78; McClellan and, 49, 51; Peninsula Campaign, 63–65; spring offensive, 93–94; victory over Lee, 80
Atlanta, Georgia, 93–94, 102–3, 125

Baker, Edward D., 53
Ball's Bluff, Virginia, 53
Baltimore, Maryland, 36–37
Banks, N. P., 78, 80, 93–94
Bates, Edward, 18, 53, 123
battles: Antietam, 66, 67; Bull Run (Manassas), first, 48–49; Bull Run (Manassas), second, 65; Chancellorsville, Virginia, 78; Chattanooga, 86; Chickamauga, 86; Fair Oaks, 64; Fredericksburg, 74, 77; Gettysburg, Pennsylvania, 80–81; Pea Ridge, Arkansas, 41; Port Hudson, Louisiana, 80, 82, 89; Seven Days, 64; Stones River, 76–77; Vicksburg, 78–80
Beauregard, P. G. T., 2–3, 48
Bell, John, 14, 20

Benjamin, Judah P., 14
Bertonneau, Arnold, 87–88
Bingham, John A., 25–26
black people, 59, 87–88, 128. *See also* Douglass, Frederick; slavery
black suffrage, 87–89, 127–28
black troops: Banks and, 80; Douglass's protest to Lincoln about discrimination against, 88–89; Lincoln to Conkling on emancipation and recruitment of, 85–86, 112–14; and prisoner-exchange agreement, 108; recruitment of, as Union-saving measure, 84; role in army and navy, 114
Blair, Frank, 18, 41
Blair, Montgomery, 18, 29, 70, 103, 123
Booth, John Wilkes, 128
Bragg, Braxton, 73–74, 76, 86
Breckinridge, John C., 20
Browning, Orville H., 54, 106
Buchanan, James, 11, 22, 30
Buell, Don Carlos, 56, 73–74
Bull Run (Manassas), 48–49, 65
Burnside, Ambrose E., 61, 73–74, 83–84
Butler, Benjamin, 93–94

Cameron, Simon, 18–19, 24, 42–43, 60, 112
Campbell, William B., 20
Chancellorsville, Virginia, 78
Chandler, Zachariah, 103
Chase, Salmon P.: and 1864 election, 91; ambition of, 93; on Buell, 74; as cabinet member, 18; Hooker's resignation and, 80; Lincoln's tolerance of, 91–93; resignation of, 75–76, 92–93; Seward's opposition to appointment of, 25; Seward's removal demanded by Republicans and, 74–76; as Supreme Court chief justice candidate, 123–24

Thomas, George H., 86, 125
Tod, David, 93
Trent crisis, 57–58
Trumbull, Lyman, 16–17

Unionist sentiment: in Upper South and Border states, 20–21
Union troops: Army of Northern Virginia, 80–81; Army of the Cumberland, 86; Army of the Ohio, 83–84; black, recruited as Union-saving measure, 84; comparison of Confederate officers to those of, 1–2; Lincoln as critical variable in victory by, 3; Massachusetts Sixth Regiment, 36–37; movement by rail, 86; naval successes, 55; New York Seventh Regiment, 37; Ohio 163rd Regiment, 115; spring offensive, 93–94; victories following Stanton's appointment as secretary of war, 61–62. *See also* Army of the Potomac (Division of the Potomac)
U.S. Congress: Joint Committee on the Conduct of the War, 55–56; Lincoln's annual message to (1861), 31, 44–47, 58; — (1862), 69; — (1863), 86–87; Lincoln's decision not to summon, 34–35; Lincoln's message to, regarding early conduct of Civil War, 37–38; retroactive approval of Lincoln's emergency measures, 47; Second Confiscation Act, 67
U.S. Constitution: proposed amendment abolishing slavery, 94, 122–23;

racial equality assumption as basis of, 13–14; on suspension of writ of habeas corpus, 38–39; Thirteenth Amendment, 25–26, 122–23
U.S. Supreme Court: chief justice candidates, 123–24; ruling on blockade, 47

Vallandigham, Clement L., 83–84, 85, 109
Vicksburg, Mississippi, 78–80
Victoria (Queen of England), 57
Virginia, 35

Wade, Benjamin F., 54, 56, 89–90
Wade-Davis Bill, 89–90
war atrocities, 109–10
War Department, 43–44, 61–62
War Orders, 62–63
war-power employed by Lincoln, 46–47
Washburne, Elihu, 93
weapons smuggling, 41
Weed, Thurlow, 111–12
Welles, Gideon, 18, 53
Wells, David A., 11–12
Whig doctrine, 44, 114–15
White, Horace, 10
white supremacy, 13
Whitney, Henry C., 9
Wilkes, Charles, 57
Wilmot Proviso, 14–15
writ of habeas corpus, suspension of, 35, 38–39

Yancy, William L., 14

Michael Burlingame, holder of the Chancellor Naomi B. Lynn Distinguished Chair in Lincoln Studies at the University of Illinois Springfield, is the author of *The Inner World of Abraham Lincoln* and *Abraham Lincoln: A Life*, which won the 2010 Lincoln Prize. He has also edited several volumes of Lincoln primary source materials, most of which have been published by Southern Illinois University Press.

CONCISE
LINCOLN
LIBRARY

This series of concise books fills a need for short studies of the life, times, and legacy of President Abraham Lincoln. Each book gives readers the opportunity to quickly achieve basic knowledge of a Lincoln-related topic. These books bring fresh perspectives to well-known topics, investigate previously overlooked subjects, and explore in greater depth topics that have not yet received book-length treatment. For a complete list of current and forthcoming titles, see www.conciselincolnlibrary.com.

Other Books in the Concise Lincoln Library

Abraham Lincoln and Horace Greeley
Gregory A. Borchard

Lincoln and the Election of 1860
Michael S. Green

Abraham and Mary Lincoln
Kenneth J. Winkle